NUTSHELLS

HUNT: A LEVEL LAW

D0542173

NUTSHELLS

HUNT: A LEVEL LAW

SECOND EDITION

by Martin Hunt, LL.B., MA,

Lecturer in Law,

Yeovil College

SWEET & MAXWELL  THOMSON REUTERS

Published in 2004 by Sweet & Maxwell, 100 Avenue Road, London NW3 3PF
part of Thomson Reuters (Professional) UK Limited
(Registered in England & Wales, Company No 1679046.
Registered Office and address for service:
Aldgate House, 33 Aldgate High Street, London EC3N 1DL)

Printed on Demand by
Hobbs the Printers, Totton, Hampshire

No natural forests were destroyed to make this product,
only farmed timber was used and replanted.

A CIP catalogue record for this book is available from the British Library

ISBN: 978 0 421 87510 4

CONTENTS

1. PRIMARY LEGISLATION

What is "primary legislation"?

Primary legislation refers to **Acts of Parliament** (or statutes). These are the most important laws in England because they are the enacted will of a sovereign Parliament. In this sense, Parliament (consisting of the House of Commons, House of Lords, and the Crown) is the highest authority in the country. Both delegated legislation and European legislation derive their validity from Acts of Parliament, and precedent (or judge-made law) is subordinate to Acts of Parliament.

What is a "Bill"?

A Bill is the formal proposal for new legislation that is debated and approved by Parliament. There are *three* types of Bill:

(1) **Public Bills** are proposals put forward by the Government and affect the general law of the land. Most new legislation results from Public Bills.
(2) **Private Members Bills** are proposals put forward by individual backbench MPs (see below).
(3) **Private Bills** are proposals that only affect a particular interest—*e.g.* to allow the development of a port or building a new railway line.

How are Acts of Parliament made?

Making a new Act of Parliament involves *four* phases:

Proposal ⇨ **Consultation** ⇨ **Drafting** ⇨ **Enactment**

Where do proposals for new Acts come from?

Most proposals come from *four* main sources:

(1) **The Government** proposes most new legislation. This may come from promises in their election manifesto, or it may be in response to an unexpected emergency (*e.g.* anti-

terrorism legislation). Most, however, emerge from discussion in government.

(2) **Advisory Agencies** also make a large number of proposals. The most important is the **Law Commission**. This was established in 1965 to keep all areas of the law under review and produce proposals for reform. There are five Commissioners. The Chairman is a High Court judge. The other four Commissioners are experienced judges, barristers, solicitors, or teachers of law. They are assisted by an administrative and research staff. In addition to producing reports and draft Bills, the Commission also produces proposals for the consolidation and codification of existing laws. Although the Commission has been responsible for a number of important law reforms (*e.g.* Children Act 1989), the 2003 Quinquennial Review showed that only around half of its reports are implemented, and the time from report to implementation is around three years. This means that some important reforms are either delayed or ignored. Another type of agency is a **Royal Commission**. Royal Commissions are established to investigate a specific issue and disband once they have reported. Again, some important reforms have been achieved in this way (*e.g.* the Police and Criminal Evidence Act 1984 resulted from the report of the Royal Commission on Criminal Procedure—the "Philips Commission"). More recently, the Government has used *informal reviews* to generate proposals for reform (*e.g.* the Halliday Review led to the sentencing reforms in the Criminal Justice Act 2003).

(3) **Pressure Groups** can also lead to law reform as a result of their campaigns. This includes both groups who campaign about a particular *cause*, such as the environment, and those who campaign on behalf of a particular *interest*, such as children or the elderly.

(4) **Individual MPs** can introduce Private Members Bills to Parliament. These are either **"Ballot Bills"** (where the MP has been successful in the annual ballot for the limited time available to debate PMBs) or **"10–Minute Rule Bills"** (which are used to raise an issue rather than actually change the law). Most PMBs are unsuccessful either because of lack of time or government opposition. Nevertheless, some important reforms have been made in this way (*e.g.* Abortion Act 1967).

What is the consultation process?

The Government will consult on its proposals for new legislation by publishing either a **Green Paper** (containing tentative proposals for discussion) or a **White Paper** (containing firm proposals for implementation). While anyone can participate by submitting their views on the proposals, most responses will come from groups directly affected (*e.g.* Headteachers' associations, the teaching unions, and parents' groups will be likely to respond to proposals in an Education White Paper).

What is the drafting process?

This is the process by which proposals for new Acts are translated into a formal Bill to be presented to Parliament. Public Bills are drafted for the Government by expert lawyers in the Parliamentary Counsel Office. This is a very important process because any errors or lack of clarity in drafting can cause problems of interpretation for the courts later on.

What is the enactment process?

This is the process by which Parliament debates and approves the Bill, making it an Act of Parliament. This involves a number of stages:

(1) **First Reading**—a purely formal stage to introduce the Bill with no debate. Bills can be introduced into either the Commons or Lords, but most important or controversial Bills start in the Commons.

(2) **Second Reading**—a general debate on the main principles and purpose of the Bill.

(3) **Committee Stage**—here the Bill is scrutinised in detail and amended by a small group of MPs or (in the case of constitutional bills) by the whole House sitting as a committee.

(4) **Report Stage**—the Committee reports its proceedings to the full House. Amendments made are accepted or rejected and further amendments considered.

(5) **Third Reading**—a final general debate on the Bill in its amended form.

(6) **Other House**—the Bill passes to the Other House where stages (1)–(5) are repeated. Any further amendments are referred back to the originating House.

(7) **Royal Assent**—having been agreed by both Houses, the Bill is sent to the monarch for Royal Assent. In modern times, this is a formality. It was last refused by Queen Anne in 1707. Following Royal Assent, the Bill is now an Act of Parliament.

What happens if the Commons and Lords disagree?

On the rare occasions where the Commons and Lords cannot agree on a compromise version of a Bill, the Commons (as the directly elected chamber) can use its powers under the Parliament Acts 1911 and 1949 to send the Bill directly to the Crown for Royal Assent. This has only happened on four occasions since 1945—*e.g.* Sexual Offences (Amendment) Act 2000). This emphasises that the role of the Lords is as a revising chamber, suggesting changes and improvements, rather than a rival chamber to the Commons.

2. DELEGATED LEGISLATION

What is "delegated legislation"?

Delegated legislation is law made by individuals (*e.g.* government ministers) or institutions (*e.g.* local councils) acting under a grant of legislative authority from Parliament. Parliament grants this authority in an enabling or parent Act. The Act will establish a framework of general principles and then delegate authority to others to fill in the details. For example, the Health and Safety at Work Act 1974 created a general framework of health and safety principles and then delegated authority to government ministers to issue detailed regulations for specific industries.

What types of delegated legislation are there?

There are *three* main types of delegated legislation:

(1) **Statutory Instruments**—these are rules, regulations and orders issued by government ministers (*e.g.* health and safety regulations). They are national in effect. Approximately 3000 are issued each year.

(2) **Byelaws**—these are laws made by local councils, regulating matters such as behaviour in public parks. They can also be issued by some corporations (*e.g.* by London Transport to ban smoking on the Underground). They are local in effect, limited to the area controlled by the issuing authority.

(3) **Orders in Council**—these are the least common type, and are issued by the Privy Council. They are most suitable for a quick response to a national emergency.

Why do we need delegated legislation?

Delegated legislation is necessary because:

(1) it **saves parliamentary time**, leaving Parliament free to debate and decide major questions of policy without getting bogged down in the detail;

(2) it **is able to deal effectively with complex and technical issues** by enabling the involvement of experts with knowledge and skills that Parliament does not have;

(3) it **enables the efficient amendment and up-dating of the law** to respond to technological, economic and other changes, without having to go through the time-consuming process of passing an amending Act. For example, while the basic principles of health and safety contained in the 1974 Act have remained the same, the detailed regulations for particular industries need to be reviewed and up-dated on regular basis. This also means that delegated legislation **allows a prompt response to emergencies;** and

(4) it allows, through byelaws, for **local variations in the law to meet specific local or institutional needs**.

Are there any disadvantages to delegated legislation?

The main disadvantage is that by transferring legislative authority from Parliament (the Legislature) to national and local government (the Executive), those making delegated legislation **may not be adequately accountable for what they do and may be able to misuse their authority**. This is why a series of checks and controls have been put in place.

What checks and controls are there?

There are *three* main forms of control:

(1) **Consultation**—the enabling Act usually requires consultation before use of the delegated authority (*e.g.* before issuing health and safety regulations, the minister must consult with those working in the industry concerned). This acts as a check both *directly* (by requiring the authority to be used openly) and *indirectly* (as a failure to consult may lead to a successful challenge in the courts—see (3) below).

(2) **Parliamentary Oversight**—this may seem odd as one of the main reasons for delegated legislation is to save parliamentary time. Nevertheless, Parliament must use some time to monitor delegated legislation, otherwise delegation becomes abdication. All statutory instruments are referred to the Scrutiny Committee (a small group of MPs and Peers) for a technical review. The Committee will report any which seem badly drafted or seem to exceed the power. However, the committee cannot consider an instrument's policy merits. This has led the Hansard Society to recommend that instruments should also be considered by the relevant departmental select committee, adding a 'policy filter' to the 'technical filter' provided by the Scrutiny Committee. After scrutiny, most instruments also have to be affirmed (or approved) by Parliament. In order save time, most instruments only need "negative" affirmation (*i.e.* they come into force unless Parliament objects). However, some instruments dealing with very important issues (*e.g.* those using a 'Henry VIII power' to make changes to primary legislation) need "positive" affirmation (*i.e.* they do not come into force unless Parliament expressly approves them).

(3) **Judicial Review**—because of the specific and limited nature of delegated legislative authority, the courts can annul delegated legislation if that authority has been exceeded (*i.e.* if the legislation is *ultra vires*). "Substantive" *ultra vires* is where the subject-matter of the legislation is beyond the scope of the power (*e.g. Attorney-General v Fulham Corporation* [1921]—a power to establish public wash-houses did not allow the establishment of public laundries). "Procedural" *ultra vires* is where there has been a serious failure to comply with a mandatory procedural requirement (*e.g.* a failure to consult or inadequate consultation—*Agricultural Training Board v Aylesbury Mushrooms* [1972]). The courts may also annul

delegated legislation where it is incompatible with a convention right under the Human Rights Act 1998. However, the cost and time involved in court action can limit the effectiveness of judicial review as a method of control.

3. EUROPEAN LEGISLATION

What is the European Union?

The European Union was created after the Second World War to help with the post-war economic and physical reconstruction of Europe and help prevent future European wars. Britain did not join until 1973. In order to achieve its objectives, the Union had to establish its own governing institutions and law—a European Legal Order.

What are the institutions of the Union?

There are *five* main Union institutions:

(1) **European Council**—made up of the Heads of Government and Foreign Ministers of the Member States, the Council takes the major decisions on the future of the Union.

(2) **Council of Ministers**—the main decision-making and legislative body. It is the Council of Ministers that adopts (enacts) most Union legislation following proposals by the Commission.

(3) **Commission**—the main executive body. Headed by the President of the Union and the Union Commissioners (each with responsibility for specific issues, such as transport), the Commission is responsible for the administration of the Union. It also proposes most Union legislation and has minor legislative powers of its own.

(4) **Parliament**—consisting of directly-elected MPs from the Member States, the Parliament has a largely consultative and advisory role, rather than being a legislative body similar to the UK Parliament.

(5) **Court of Justice**—staffed by judges nominated by the Member States, the Court of Justice (assisted by the Court of First Instance) has both an *administrative jurisdiction* (hearing actions against Union institutions and Member States, and reviewing the validity of Union legislation), and a *constitutional jurisdiction* (providing definitive interpretations of Union law in response to questions referred to it by national courts of the Member States).

How does Union law relate to the national law of Member States?

Some forms of Union law are said to be **directly applicable**. This means they are automatically part of the law of the Member States without the need for national legislation. Some Union law is also **directly effective**. This means it creates individual rights that can be enforced in national courts. This can be either *vertical* direct effect (creating individual rights against the State) or *horizontal* direct effect (creating rights against other individuals).

What are the different types of Union law?

There are *four* main types of Union law:

(1) **Treaties**—because they establish the main principles of the Union, its governing rules and institutions, and how it will make laws, the treaties function as the Union's constitution. Treaty provisions are *not* directly applicable, but can have both vertical and horizontal direct effect provided they are clear, precise, and unconditional (*Van Gend en Loos* [1963]). The three forms of Union legislation (see (2)–(4) below) are identified in Article 249 of the Treaty of Rome.

(2) **Regulations**—as regulations *are* directly applicable and binding in their entirety, they cannot be varied or amended by national legislation, creating legislative *uniformity* across the Union. They can have both vertical and horizontal direct effect provided the "Van Gend" requirements are met (*Leonesio v Italian Ministry of Agriculture* [1973]).

(3) **Directives**—these are *not* directly applicable, and being binding only as to the result to be achieved, they leave the form and method of implementation to each Member

State, creating legislative *harmony* across the Union. They can have vertical direct effect *only*, provided the "Van Gend" reguirements are met (*Van Duyn v Home Office* [1974]) and the time limit for implementation has expired (*Marshall v Southampton and SW Hants AHA* [1986]; *Faccini Dori v Recreb* [1994]). This means an individual cannot rely on a Directive against another individual, although there are three ways round this restriction:

(a) **Indirect effect**—when interpreting national legislation, national courts must do so in a way that complies with directive rights (*Von Colson* [1984]; *Marleasing* [1990]).

(b) **State liability in damages**—an individual can claim damages from the State where: (a) the directive was intended to create individual rights; (b) those rights are precisely specified; (c) the Member State's failure to implement the directive caused the individual's loss (*Francovitch v Italy* [1993]).

(c) **Incidental horizontal direct effect**—where the court has to refer to the directive in order to resolve a dispute between individuals under national law (*Unilever v Central Foods* [2000]).

(4) **Decisions**—while *not* directly applicable, decisions are binding on their entirety on those to whom they are addressed (whether a Member State, company, or an individual). A decision may have vertical direct effect *only*, provided the "Van Gend" requirements are met and it is addressed to a Member State (*Grad v Finanzamt Traunstein* [1970]).

Has Union membership affected the sovereignty of the UK Parliament?

The **Union view** is very clear. According to the Court of Justice, if the aims of the Union are to be achieved, Union law must prevail over inconsistent national law, and by joining the Union, Member States permanently transfer part of their sovereignty to the Union (*Costa v ENEL* [1964]). National courts must, therefore, disapply inconsistent national law (*Minister of Finance v Simmenthal* [1978]).

The **UK view** is less certain. The European Communities Act 1972, s.2(4), enacts a modified version of the "Costa" position, providing that all UK legislation takes effect subject to Union law with the exception of the 1972 Act itself. Theoretically, therefore, the UK Parliament could reassert its full sovereignty by amending or repealing the 1972 Act. This is extremely unlikely, and in the meantime the position seems to be:

(1) The UK courts will seek to resolve any inconsistency through interpretation (*Garland v BR Engineering* [1982]).

(2) If Parliament wishes to enact legislation contrary to Union law, it must first expressly amend or repeal the 1972 Act, otherwise the courts will continue to give priority to Union law (*Macarthys v Smith* [1979]). This is because, as a constitutional statute, the 1972 Act is entrenched against implied repeal (*Thoburn v Sunderland CC* [2002]).

(3) In exceptional circumstances, the court may suspend the operation of UK legislation while waiting for guidance from the Court of Justice on an apparent inconsistency (*Factortame (No.2)* [1990]).

What is the relationship between the UK courts and the Court of Justice?

Under Article 234 of the Treaty of Rome, any national court *can* refer a question of Union law to the Court of Justice for a *preliminary ruling* where a ruling is necessary to enable it to decide the case. If the court is one from which there is no appeal under national law (*e.g.* the House of Lords), then in such circumstances it *must* make a reference. In deciding whether a ruling is necessary, the UK courts use the *Bulmer v Bollinger* [1974] guidelines (*e.g.* a ruling is not necessary where Court of Justice has previously ruled on the point, or where the point is reasonably clear and free from doubt—the *acte clair* doctrine). The national court will then decide the case in light of the ruling from the Court of Justice—*i.e.* while Union law is *interpreted* by the Court of Justice, it is *applied* by the national courts of the Member States.

4. STATUTORY INTERPRETATION

Why is statutory interpretation necessary?

The courts have to interpret legislation in order to resolve disputes over the meaning or scope of particular words and phrases. Because of the pressure of time on those drafting legislation, the complexity of the subject-matter, the natural ambiguity of language, the passage of time, and the fact that certain techniques (such as re-stating in different words or giving worked examples) are not available to the draftsman, it is not always clear whether or how a particular piece of legislation applies to a particular situation. For example, is a 'Go-Ped' motorised scooter a 'motor vehicle' for the purposes of the Road Traffic Act 1988? (*CC of North Yorks v Saddington* [2000].)

How do the courts approach the interpretation of legislation?

There are *three* traditional approaches to the interpretation of legislation:

(1) **Literal approach**—here the words are given their ordinary, literal meaning *even if* the outcome is absurd or repugnant (see, for example, *Whiteley v Chappell* [1868]; *Fisher v Bell* [1960]). If the outcome is absurd or repugnant, the solution lies in parliamentary amendment, not judicial interpretation (*R v Judge of the City of London Court* [1892]).

(2) **Golden approach**—here the words are given their ordinary, literal meaning *unless* the outcome is absurd or repugnant, in which case a more suitable alternative meaning will be given (see, for example, *R v Allen* [1872]; *Adler v George* [1964]).

(3) **Mischief (or Modern Purposive) approach**—here the words are given the meaning most likely to advance the purpose of the legislation or the intention of Parliament. The mischief approach stated in *Heydon's Case* [1584] has evolved into the modern purposive approach (see, for example, *Smith v Hughes* [1960]). Under a purposive approach, while the courts may, in exceptional circumstances, even add, delete, or substitute words, they must

be careful not to cross the boundary between legitimate judicial interpretation and unwarranted judicial legislation, preserving the proper constitutional balance between Parliament and the courts (*Jones v Wrotham Park Estates* [1979]; *Inco Europe v First Choice Distribution* [2000]).

In more recent times, rather than choose between these traditional approaches, the courts have merged elements from each into the *Modern Unitary Approach*. Here the courts will take into account the literal meaning of the words, the context in which they are used, and the purpose underlying the provision in which they appear. Of these three elements (words, context, and purpose), greater weight tends to be given to the purposive (see, for example, *Re Attorney-General's Reference (No.1) [1988]*).

Are there any other guidelines the courts use?

The courts also use a number of *rules of language* and *presumptions* when interpreting legislation. Two of the more important rules of language are:

(1) *Ejusdem generis*—this rule means that where general words follow a list of specific words, the general take their meaning from the specific (*e.g.* cats, dogs, and other animals would apply to all domestic animals, but not wild animals or livestock).

(2) *Expressio unius exclusio alterius*—this rule means that the express inclusion of one member of a particular class excludes, by implication, those members not mentioned (*e.g.* quarries and coal mines would apply to all types of quarry, but only to coal mines and not to any other type of mine).

Among the more significant presumptions are those of mens rea in criminal statutes and against retrospective effect.

The courts are also bound to try to interpret UK legislation in a way that is compatible with European Union law (*Von Colson* [1984]; *Marleasing* [1990]), and in a way that is compatible with the European Convention on Human Rights (Human Rights Act 1998, s.3).

What are the strengths and weaknesses of these different approaches?

The advantages claimed for the literal approach are that it promotes certainty, reduces litigation, and is constitutionally correct. However, against this it can be said that it ignores the natural ambiguity of language and the inevitable imperfection of drafting. Furthermore, it assumes that the literal meaning is *always* the correct one—while it is *often* so, it is not *automatically* so. Finally, it takes a rather narrow and legalistic view of parliamentary sovereignty, assuming that if the outcome of the literal meaning is absurd or repugnant, then this must be what Parliament intended.

The main advantage claimed for the golden approach is that it avoids the most absurd or repugnant consequences of following a strictly literal approach. However, it does not make clear *how* absurd or repugnant the consequences have to be in order to justify abandoning the literal meaning. Nor does it indicate how a more suitable alternative should be selected. It is, according to Professor Zander, an "unpredictable safety valve".

The main arguments for using a purposive approach are that it is a realistic approach, acknowledging that the courts are being creative when they interpret legislation, and that they should exercise that creativity in a way that supports the purpose of the legislation, thereby paying due respect to the sovereignty of Parliament. While giving greater weight to the purposive element is, therefore, the most sensible approach to take, it is not always easy for the courts to identify the purpose of the legislation.

What can the courts look at in order to discover the intention of Parliament?

There are a number of *intrinsic (internal)* and *extrinsic (external)* aids the courts can consider:

(1) **Intrinsic material** is information contained within the statute itself. In addition to the disputed word or phrase, the courts *can* consider the longs and short title, the preamble, the headings, and the schedules. They *cannot*, however, refer to the marginal notes.

(2) **Extrinsic material** is information in sources other than the Act itself. The courts *can* consider:
   (a) Other statutes.
   (b) Official publications directly related to the enactment of the statute in question (*e.g.* Green and White Papers, Law Commission reports).
   (c) Any relevant international treaties or conventions.

(d) Hansard (the official record of parliamentary debates) but only where: (a) the statutory words are unclear, ambiguous or the literal meaning produces an absurdity; (b) the parliamentary statement is made by the minister or other promoter of the Bill; (c) the words of the statement are clear (*Pepper v Hart* [1993]). For a long time the courts were not allowed to consider Hansard. Despite the views of Lord Denning in the Court of Appeal, the House of Lords in *Davis v Johnson* [1979] took the view that there was a fundamental difference between a political debate in Parliament and the unbiased examination of a court. They were also concerned that allowing reference to Hansard would increase costs and delays. However, in *Pepper v Hart*, the House of Lords used the 1966 Practice Statement to depart from *Davis v Johnson* and, since the relaxation of the exclusionary rule, their earlier fears have proved unfounded.

The courts *cannot* consider official publications not directly related to the enactment of the statute, nor any unofficial documents (*e.g.* pressure group reports). The Law Commission published a report on the interpretation of legislation in 1969. Its most significant recommendation was that a new explanatory memorandum be published alongside the Act for the guidance of the courts and the public. This was finally implemented in 1999 with the expansion and publication of the Explanatory Notes produced for MPs. This additional information and guidance should make it easier for both the public and the courts to understand the purpose of the legislation and interpret it accordingly.

5. PRECEDENT

What does "binding precedent" mean?

Binding precedent means that a later court is bound to apply the same principles and reasoning as an earlier court where the two cases raise the same point of law. This is known as the principle of *stare decisis* (stand by the decision), and ensures that judicial decisions are based upon reason and principle. Where there is no existing precedent to follow or modify, then the court will return to first principles of justice and fairness in order to set an original precedent.

What does the legal system need to operate a system of precedent?

The operation of a system of precedent requires *three* elements to be present:

(1) A **court hierarchy** is required to establish which decisions are binding on which courts. The highest court is the House of Lords, whose decisions bind all lower courts. Next in the hierarchy is the Court of Appeal, whose Civil Division decisions bind all lower civil courts, and Criminal Division decisions bind all lower criminal courts. Below the Court of Appeal are the Divisional Courts  and the High Court, who can also establish precedents. At the bottom of the hierarchy are the Crown Courts, County Courts, and magistrates' courts, who cannot establish precedents.

(2) Accurate **law reporting** is required to enable decisions to be recorded, collated, and accessed by future courts. Modern law reporting dates from the establishment of the Council on Law Reporting in 1865 which, as the Incorporated Council, still publishes the Law Reports today. There are also important series of private reports, the best known being the *All England Law Reports*. Reports are also published in newspapers and journals (*e.g. The Times, the New Law Journal*). The most recent development has be the use of computerised reporting systems (*e.g.* All England Direct, BAILII etc) on the Internet.

(3) Rules are also required to identify the **binding element** in a decision. The binding element is known as the *ratio decidendi* (reason for the decision). This is the rule(s) of

law the judge used to reach the decision. The decision will also contain discussion of legal rules raised in argument, but not used to reach the decision. This is known as *obiter dicta* (other things said), and while it can be *persuasive* in the future, it is never binding. Other forms of *persuasive authorities* include decisions of the Privy Council, decisions of other Common Law countries (*e.g.* Australia, Canada), and academic writing.

How can you have a system of binding precedent AND allow the law to develop?

The law must be certain so that people can plan their affairs and lawyers advise their clients. It must also be flexible so that it can evolve to meet changing times. Too much certainty and the law becomes rigid and stagnant. Too much flexibility and it becomes unstable. So the system needs to achieve a balance between these two competing but legitimate aims.

Rigidity ← Certainty   Flexibility → Instability
△

The binding nature of the ratio creates a foundation of certainty. Flexibility is introduced in *three* ways:

(1) Higher courts can *overrule or reverse* the decisions of lower courts.
(2) Lower court can *distinguish* from the precedents of higher courts. This means identifying a material difference between the instant case and precedent case that justifies applying different principles (see, for example, the development of the law on marital rape—*R v R (Rape—marital exemption)* [1991]). However, lower courts can misuse this principle to avoid unwelcome precedents (see, for example, *Lewis v Averay* [1972]). Courts may also distinguish from their own previous decisions.
(3) In certain circumstances, a court can *depart* from its own previous decisions. Under the 1966 Practice Statement, the House of Lords can depart from their own previous decisions when it appears "right to do so". In considering this, the House should take into account the risk of disturbing existing civil arrangements and the particular need for certainty in the criminal law. Because of this, and because it would cause undue uncertainty if the highest court changed its opinions too often, the House has used

the Practice Statement sparingly. Nevertheless, there have been some important cases where it has been used—*e.g. R v Shivpuri* [1986] (see Chapter 20), *R v Howe* [1987] (see Chapter 15), *Pepper v Hart* [1993] (see Chapter 4), and *Arthur Hall & Co v Simons* [2000] (see Chapter 11).

The **Court of Appeal (Civil Division)** is bound by its own previous decisions, subject to the **three exceptions** identified in *Young v Bristol Aeroplane Co* [1944]: (a) where there are two conflicting previous decisions; (b) where there is subsequent and conflicting legislation or House of Lords decision; (c) where the previous decision was given *per incuriam*—in ignorance or forgetfulness of relevant legislation or precedent (*Morelle v Wakeling* [1955]). The Criminal Division is also bound subject to the 'Bristol Aeroplane' exceptions, and the exception in *R v Taylor* [1950]—it is not bound where the law was previously misapplied or misunderstood resulting in a conviction, and to follow it would therefore create an obvious injustice. This additional flexibility is because the Criminal Division is dealing with the liberty of the citizen.

In *Davis v Johnson* [1978], Lord Denning in the Court of Appeal argued that the Court of Appeal should have the same flexibility as the House of Lords. He argued that the House might never get the opportunity to correct the law, and even if it did, this could take a long time. Therefore, justice could be delayed or denied. However, the House of Lords disagreed, stating that the Practice Statement applied only to the House and did not alter precedent in relation to any other court. Lord Diplock argued that there was a fundamental difference between a court of last resort (such as the House of Lords) and an intermediate appeal court (such as the Court of Appeal), and that to extend the operation of the Practice Statement to the Court of Appeal would create uncertainty.

What are the advantages and disadvantages of a system of precedent?

Advantages:

- ☑ It is a **just** system, ensuring similar cases are decided by similar principles.
- ☑ It is an **impartial** system, requiring decisions to be made according to established principles.

☑ It provides a **practical character** to the law, allowing it to develop in response to actual cases, rather than on an exclusively theoretical basis.

☑ It provides a **degree of certainty**, allowing individuals to order their affairs and lawyers to advise their clients.

☑ It **allows a measure of flexibility**—within the binding framework of stare decisis, the hierarchy of courts, the appellate process, the provisions of the Practice Statement, the Bristol Aeroplane and R v Taylor exceptions, and distinguishing all allow the common law to evolve to meet changing times.

Disadvantages:

☒ There is a danger of **rigidity**, whereby necessary changes cannot occur because: (a) the system is contingent—changes depend upon appropriate cases reaching sufficiently superior courts (sometimes referred to as the "accidents of litigation"); (b) the retrospective effect of overruling can discourage courts from changing the law.

☒ It is a **complex** system: (a) keeping track of valid authorities and the exceptions established through distinguishing is difficult; (b) it can be difficult to identify the precise ratio of a decision, particularly in the multiple judgements of the House of Lords and Court of Appeal.

---

6. POLICE POWERS

What are the powers of the police to stop and search suspects?

The police have no powers at common law to stop people in the street or require them to answer questions (*Rice v Connolly* [1966]; *Kenlin v Gardiner* [1967]). However, under the Police Reform Act 2002, s.50, if an officer has reason to believe someone has been or is acting in an anti-social manner (a manner likely to cause harassment, alarm or distress), they can require that person to give their name and address. The main police powers of stop and search are statutory:

(1) **Police and Criminal Evidence Act 1984, s.1**, allows the police to stop and search someone where they have reasonable grounds to suspect that person is carrying stolen property or prohibited articles (*i.e.* offensive weapons, articles for use in robbery or burglary, articles for use in criminal damage). The officer must give their name and the station at which they are based, and state the purpose and legal basis for the search (PACE, s.2). The suspect cannot be required to remove any clothing in a public place other than an outer coat, jacket, and gloves (PACE, s.2). The suspect is entitled to a written record of the search (PACE, s.3). The officer may use reasonable force to carry out the search (PACE, s.117).

(2) **Criminal Justice and Public Order Act 1994, s.60**, allows a senior officer to authorise a general stop and search operation for 24 hours (with a possible 24 hour extension) in a given area if they have reasonable grounds to believe serious violence is likely. The authorisation allows officers to stop and search anyone (there is no need for reasonable suspicion) for knives or offensive weapons.

(3) **Terrorism Act 2000, s.44**, allows a senior officer to authorise a general stop and search operation in a given area if they consider it expedient for the prevention of terrorism. The authorisation (valid for 48 hours but capable of extension for up to 28 days by the Home Secretary) allows officers to stop and search anyone (there is no need for reasonable suspicion) for articles that could be used in connection with terrorism. The suspect can be required to remove headgear, footwear, an outer coat, jacket or gloves in a public place.

(4) **Miscellaneous statutory powers**—a number of other statutes (*e.g.* Misuse of Drugs Act 1971) grant specific stop and search powers, generally based on a requirement of reasonable suspicion.

What are the powers of the police to arrest suspects?

The police may obtain an **arrest warrant** from a magistrate. This tends to be used for known suspects and for those who fail to surrender to bail. The police may also **arrest without a warrant** in certain circumstances:

(1) **PACE**, s.24, allows an officer to arrest someone without a warrant if they reasonably suspect that person has committed, is committing, or is about to commit an arrestable

offence (*e.g.* one punishable by at least five years imprisonment).

(2) **PACE**, s.25 (the "general arrest conditions"), allows an officer to arrest someone without a warrant if they reasonably suspect has committed, is committing, or is about to commit any offence AND the service of a summons is inappropriate or impractical because: (a) the suspect refuses to give their name and address, the officer reasonably suspects the name or address given to be false, or the address is unsuitable for the service of a summons; or (b) the arrest is necessary to prevent harm to property, other persons, or the suspect themselves.

(3) **PACE**, s.26, preserves the common law power of the police to arrest for a breach of the peace.

(4) **Miscellaneous statutory powers**—a number of other statutes (*e.g.* Public Order Act 1986) give the police specific powers of arrest.

The suspect must be informed of the fact and reason for their arrest at the time or as soon as possible thereafter (PACE, s.28). The police may use reasonable force to carry out the arrest (PACE, s.117).

How effective are the safeguards for the suspect in these circumstances?

The use of stop and search powers under PACE is subject to guidance in **Code of Practice A**. A new Code A (effective from April 2003) prohibited the use of "voluntary" searches to circumvent PACE, requiring that all searches (except of those entering a sports ground or other premises where consent to the search is a condition of entry) must have a legal basis. It also strengthened the guidance on reasonable suspicion, stating that it must normally be linked to current and accurate intelligence or information. However, despite this, and the fact that reasonable suspicion cannot be based on personal factors alone (*e.g.* colour, race, or criminal record), there are still concerns that those from certain ethnic groups are far more likely to stopped and searched than others—Home Office statistics for 2002 show that black people are eight times more likely to stopped and searched, and Asian people three times more likely, than whites. Furthermore, the growing use of general stop and search authorisations under CJPOA, s.60 and TA, s.44, on an almost routine basis in some areas enables the police to avoid the requirement of reasonable suspicion under PACE. Also, while the courts have discretion under PACE, s.78, to exclude evidence obtained improperly where it would have an adverse effect on the fairness of the proceedings, there are concerns over inconsistencies in the exercise of this discretion. Finally, although an aggrieved suspect can make a complaint, there have also been concerns over the effectiveness and independence of the complaints system. In an attempt to address this, the Police Complaints Authority (PCA) was replaced by a new Independent Police Complaints Commission (IPCC) in April 2004 (Police Reform Act 2002, s.9).

What are the powers of the police to detain suspects at the police station?

Once the suspect has been arrested, they must be taken to a police station as soon as is practicable (PACE, s.30), unless they are granted "street bail" (Criminal Justice Act 2003, s.4). Once at the station, the suspect becomes the responsibility of the Custody Officer (CO). The CO must decide whether the suspect should be charged, released (with or without bail), or detained. A suspect can only be detained where the CO has reasonable grounds to believe that this is necessary to secure or preserve evidence, including through questioning (PACE, s.37). Any detention without charge should not last more than 24 hours (PACE, s.41), and the CO must review the necessity of the detention after no longer than six hours, and at no longer than nine hour intervals thereafter (PACE, s.40). A senior officer can authorise an extension of the detention for up to 36 hours in relation to any arrestable offence (PACE, s.42, CJA, s.7). Any extension beyond 36 hours (up to a maximum of 96 hours) must be authorised by a magistrate (PACE, ss.43, 44). Only around 1 per cent of suspects are in fact detained without charge beyond 24 hours. While detained, the suspect may be searched and samples taken (PACE, ss.54, 63), and their fingerprints may be taken (PACE, s.61). Intimate searches and samples must be authorised by a senior officer (PACE, s.62) and must be conducted by a doctor or nurse (PACE, ss.55, 62).

How effective are the safeguards for the suspect in this situation?

The use of powers of detention and questioning under PACE is subject to guidance in **Code of Practice C**. The suspect must be cautioned before questioning, and any questioning must take place in a comfortable, well-lit and ventilated interview room, with adequate rest and comfort breaks. All interviews must be tape-recorded (PACE, s.60). The suspect has the right to have someone informed of their arrest (PACE, s.56) and to receive legal advice, free of charge if necessary (PACE, s.58). However, both of these rights may be delayed for up to 36 hours by a senior officer in relation to a serious arrestable offence where they have reasonable grounds to believe that it could result in interference with evidence or witnesses, alerting of suspects still at large, or hinder the recovery of property. As noted above, the CO must review regularly the necessity of the detention, and must also maintain an accurate custody record, and conduct a risk assessment of all detainees (*e.g.* whether they require medical attention). Under Code C, any interview of a child or vulnerable adult must be conducted in the presence of an appropriate adult (*e.g.* parent or social worker). In addition to their discretion to exclude evidence improperly obtained (see above), the courts must exclude confession evidence obtained by oppressive means (PACE, s.76). An aggrieved suspect may complain to the new IPCC (see above). The Police Reform Act 2002, s.51 also provided for Independent Custody Visitors to review custody suite facilities and meet with detainees to discuss the treatment and conditions. The main concern relating to detention and questioning is whether the central and vital role of the CO is sustainable. In order to carry out their duties effectively, the CO may have to override the views of investigating officers and other police colleagues, who will necessarily have more information available to them, and may well be more senior in rank (especially in relation to serious offences where extended detention may be necessary). Therefore, there is a risk that the CO will simply 'rubber stamp' decisions made by the investigating officers.

7. CRIMINAL PROCESS

What happens when a suspect is charged?

Following arrest, and possible detention and questioning, the suspect must be either charged or released. Following pilot studies that showed a significant increase in convictions and guilty pleas, the Criminal Justice Act 2003 provides for a greater role for the Crown Prosecution Service, alongside the police, in the charging of suspects. Following charge, the suspect will either be detained in custody or released on bail. The Custody Officer must release the suspect (with or without bail) unless they have substantial grounds to believe that the suspect will fail to surrender to bail, commit further offences, interfere with witnesses, or otherwise obstruct the course of justice.

What is the role of the magistrates' court?

The role of the magistrates' court is to try summary offences, send to the Crown Court for trial those charged with indictable offences, and determine whether those charged with "either-way" offences are tried at the magistrates' or Crown Court. Once a suspect has been charged, they are brought before the magistrates' court for an Early Administrative Hearing, when applications for bail and legal aid are dealt with, and any necessary reports (*e.g.* medical reports) ordered.

How do magistrates decide whether or not the defendant will be granted bail?

Under the Bail Act 1976, s.4, there is a general right to bail, no matter how serious the offence charged. However, under Schedule 1 of the Act, magistrates can refuse bail where there are substantial grounds to believe that the defendant (D) will fail to surrender to bail, commit further offences, interfere with witnesses, or otherwise obstruct the course of justice, or where the alleged offence was committed while on bail for another offence. In deciding this, the court must take into account the nature and seriousness of the offence, the character, antecedents, associations and community ties of D, D's previous record of answering to bail, and the strength of the evidence. Also, bail need not be granted where D needs to be kept in custody for their own protection or welfare. Bail can be granted subject to conditions (*e.g.* to report to the police, reside at a particular address, abide by a curfew), and may be subject to a financial security (provided by D) or surety (provided by a third party) which is forfeit if D absconds. Under the Bail (Amendment) Act 1993 (as amended by CJA 2003), the prosecution can appeal against a grant of bail where D is charged with an imprisonable offence.

Also, under the Criminal Justice and Public Order Act 1994 (as amended by the Crime and Disorder Act 1998), where D is charged with a specified serious offence (*e.g.* rape) and has a previous conviction for such an offence, then bail may only be granted in exceptional circumstances.

How do the magistrates decide whether an "either-way" offence is tried at the magistrates' court or the Crown Court?

Regarding "either-way" offences, the magistrates' court will proceed to the *plea before venue* stage. Under the Criminal Procedure and Investigation Act 1996, if D indicates a guilty plea, they lose the right to a Crown Court trial, and the magistrates dispose of the case summarily. This can include committing D for sentencing at the Crown Court if the magistrates believe their sentencing powers are inadequate. If D indicates that he intends to plead not guilty, the magistrates must determine whether summary trial or trial on indictment is appropriate, although D may elect for trial on indictment. Trials at the magistrates' court are quicker and cheaper than those at the Crown Court, and, from D's point of view, there are lower possible penalties, although this must be balanced against a greater chance of conviction. Crown Court trials take longer, may be delayed and are more expensive, while from D's point of view the advantages of a greater chance of acquittal and better legal representation must be weighed against the possibility of a higher sentence if convicted—judges are three times more likely than magistrates to impose an immediate custodial sentence, and that sentence is on average two and a half times as long as those imposed by magistrates.

What is the role of the Youth Court?

Apart from those charged with the most serious offences, young defendants (between 10 and 17) are tried by magistrates sitting as a Youth Court. The magistrates receive special training for this role. The hearings are far less formal than those in an adult court and are held in private. Reporting restrictions mean the media cannot identify the defendant even if convicted unless the court allows. This is a particularly important court as the peak age for offending is 17–18. The idea underlying a special court with an informal approach and reporting restrictions is to keep young offenders apart from adult offenders and maximise the possibility that early, sensitive and appropriate intervention will prevent the individual becoming trapped in a cycle of offending.

What are the routes of appeal for the defendant?

Appeals from summary conviction at the magistrates' court lie to either:

(1) The Crown Court. Where D pleaded guilty, they can only appeal against sentence. Where the plea was not guilty, they may appeal against conviction, sentence or both. The Crown Court can confirm, reverse or vary the decision of the magistrates (including increasing the sentence) or remit the case back to the magistrates' court with its opinion. Further appeal on a point of law can be made to the Queen's Bench Divisional Court by way of case stated.
(2) Alternatively, either the defence or prosecution can appeal directly, by way of case stated, from the magistrates' court to the Queen's Bench Divisional Court. The Divisional Court can confirm, reverse or vary the decision of the magistrates or remit the case back to the magistrates' court with its opinion.

Further appeal lies from the Divisional Court to the House of Lords provided the Divisional Court certifies that the appeal raises a point of law of general public importance and the Divisional Court or the House of Lords grants permission on the basis that the point of law is one which ought to be considered by the House of Lords (Administration of Justice Act 1960, s.1).

Appeal from conviction on indictment at the Crown Court to the Court of Appeal (Criminal Division) is possible where either the trial judge grants an appeal certificate or the Court of Appeal grants permission to appeal (Criminal Appeal Act 1995, s.1). D can appeal against sentence, conviction or both, regardless of plea at trial. When dealing with an appeal against conviction only, the Court of Appeal has no power to interfere with the sentence passed by the Crown Court. The Court of Appeal must allow an appeal against conviction where it is satisfied that the conviction is unsafe (Criminal Appeal Act 1995, s.2). Regarding an appeal against sentence, the Court of Appeal may confirm, vary or reduce the sentence imposed by the Crown Court—it cannot increase the sentence. It may also use the opportunity to provide sentencing guidelines for the Crown Court.

Further appeal, by either the defence or prosecution, lies from the Court of Appeal to the House of Lords provided the Court of Appeal certifies that the appeal raises a point of law of general public importance and the Court of Appeal or House of Lords grants permission to appeal on the basis that the point of law is one which ought to be considered by the House of Lords (Criminal Appeal Act 1968, s.33).

Can the prosecution appeal against either acquittal or sentence?

Following summary trial in the magistrates' court, the prosecution can appeal by way of case-stated on a point of law to the Queen's Bench Divisional Court. While the prosecution cannot appeal generally against an acquittal in the Crown Court, the Attorney General can refer questions on a point of law to the Court of Appeal (Criminal Justice Act 1972, s.36). While the opinion of the Court of Appeal has no effect on the acquittal, this is an important mechanism for resolving doubtful points of criminal law. The Court of Appeal may refer the question on to the House of Lords. Furthermore, the Criminal Justice Act 2003, ss.75–79, abolished the 'double jeopardy' rule for specified serious offences (*e.g.* murder, rape), allowing the Court of Appeal, following an application from the Director of Public Prosecutions, to quash an acquittal and order a retrial where there is new and compelling evidence and a retrial is in the interests of justice. Furthermore, while the prosecution cannot appeal against sentence, the Attorney General may refer the sentence to the Court of Appeal where it is thought unduly lenient (Criminal Justice Act 1988, s.36). The Court of Appeal may confirm, vary, decrease or increase the sentence, and may again use the opportunity to issue sentencing guidelines.

What is the role of the Criminal Cases Review Commission?

Once all avenues of appeal had been explored, that was the end of the matter unless the Home Secretary exercised his power to refer a case to the Court of Appeal. Successive home secretaries were reluctant to do this. Following a series of highly publicised miscarriages of justice (*e.g.* the "Guildford Four"), the Royal Commission on Criminal Justice (1993) recommended this power should pass to an independent review body and the Criminal Cases Review Commission was established in 1997 under the Criminal Appeal Act 1995. The main role of the Commission is to consider suspected miscarriages of justice, arrange investigations where appropriate, and refer cases to the Court of Appeal where necessary. In its first Annual Report, the Commission reported that while the initial review procedure was being completed quickly, considerable delays were occurring in dealing with those cases taken forward for detailed review. Subsequently, the Commission has reported that increases in funding have allowed it to make significant inroads into the case backlog and to reduce delays. Finally, it seems that the Commission's review and referral procedures are working well, and 65 per cent of cases referred to the Court of Appeal have resulted in the conviction being quashed:

Figures to October 31, 2003:

Total applications	6,297
Open	228
Actively being worked on	406
Completed	5,663 (including ineligible)—216 referrals
Heard by Court of Appeal	160 (104 quashed; 50 upheld; 6 reserved)

8. SENTENCING

What are the aims of sentencing?

The Criminal Justice Act 2003, s.142, states that the aims of sentencing are:

(1) the punishment of offenders;
(2) the reduction of crime (including its reduction by deterrence);
(3) the reform and rehabilitation of offenders;
(4) the protection of the public; and
(5) the making of reparation by offenders to persons affected by their offences.

Punishment reflects the idea of retribution, in that punishment means the offender receives the just desserts of their wrongdoing. Deterrence is intended to reduce crime by both discouraging the offender from further offences (individual deterrence) and, by example, discouraging others from offending (general deterrence). However, as many offences are committed in the heat of the moment, while intoxicated, or are opportunistic rather than considered, the deterrent effect of punishment should not be overestimated. Reform and rehabilitation is based on the idea that people are not inherently criminal but that they offend for a reason (see the relationship between social exclusion and offending below). The idea is that constructive penalties (*e.g.* involving education, training, or addiction programmes) will help in removing the need for offending behaviour. This is particularly important in relation to young offenders (see below). The public need to be protected from offending behaviour, and in a small minority of cases this requires lengthy custodial penalities. Finally, the idea of reparation, of making good the consequences of offending behaviour, is intended to help offenders face up to their offending and to help victims come to terms with being offended against. This can involve measures of direct benefit to the victim (restorative justice) or to the broader community.

How do these aims relate to the various sentences available?

The three main types of sentence available are **custodial** sentences, **community** sentences, and **fines**. Custodial sentences are clearly related to the aims of punishment, deterrence, and public protection, and should also ideally contain an element of rehabilitation. Community sentences are more clearly focussed on the aims of rehabilitation and reparation, though they will also have an element of punishment and deterrence. Fines are mainly concerned with punishment and deterrence, though they make an indirect form of reparation.

What are the rules on custodial sentences?

Under the CJA, s.152, a court cannot impose a custodial sentence unless the offence(s) is so serious that neither a community sentence nor a fine alone can be justified. Under s.153, the length of that sentence should be for the shortest time possible that is commensurate with the seriousness of the offence(s). This reflects the importance of the idea of *proportionality*—that both the type and severity of sentence should be proportionate to the seriousness of the offence. In *R v Cunningham* [1993], "commensurate with the seriousness of the offence" was held to mean "commensurate with the punishment and deterrence that the seriousness of the offence requires", emphasising the link between custodial sentences and these two aims of punishment.

Following concerns over the ineffectiveness of short (*i.e.* less than 12 months) prison sentences, highlighted in the Halliday Review of Sentencing (2001), the CJA created three new sentences to replace custodial sentences of less than 12 months:

(1) **Custody Plus (s.181)**—this involves a short prison sentence (between two and 13 weeks) followed by a period of community supervision of not less than 26 weeks, the total being not more than 51 weeks. The idea is that the offender receives the shock of the 'clang of the prison door,' and may therefore be more receptive to the subsequent community rehabilitation measures.

(2) **Intermittent Custody (s.183)**—this involves a short prison sentence (between 14 and 90 days) to be served intermittently, with periods of community supervision in between, the total period being not less than 28 weeks and not more than 51 weeks. Again, the idea is that the offender receives the shock of custody, but in a way that enables them to maintain family and community links that should help them avoid reoffending.

(3) **Custody Minus** (suspended sentences) **(s.189)**—where the court passes a prison sentence of between 28 and 51 weeks, it may suspend that sentence for a period of between six months and two years, while ordering the offending to follow a programme of community rehabilitation. Should the offender breach the conditions of the community programme, or re-offend within this period, then the original sentence will take effect.

In certain circumstances, the court must pass a minimum, extended or indeterminate sentence of imprisonment:

(1) **Mandatory minimums**—unless there are exceptional circumstances, the court must impose a minimum of seven years imprisonment for a third Class A drug trafficking

offence (Powers of Criminal Courts (Sentencing) Act 2000, s.110), three years for a third domestic burglary (PCCSA, s.111), and five years for certain firearms offences (CJA, s.287). Also, where a person commits a specified serious offence that is liable to life imprisonment, then a court must impose a life sentence where it is satisfied *both* that the offence(s) is sufficiently serious to justify such a sentence and that the offender represents a significant risk of serious harm to the public (CJA, s.225).

(2) **Extended sentences**—where a person commits a specified violent or sexual offence, and the court believes the offender represents a significant risk of serious harm to the public, then the court must pass an extended sentence of up to an additional five years for a violent offence and eight years for a sexual offence (CJA, s.227).

(3) **Indeterminate sentences**—where a person commits a specified serious offence that is *not* liable to life imprisonment, then a court must impose a sentence of imprisonment for public protection (*i.e.* an indeterminate sentence) where it is satisfied *both* that the offence(s) is sufficiently serious to justify such a sentence AND that the offender represents a significant risk of serious harm to the public (CJA, s.225).

What are the rules on community sentences?

Under the CJA, s.148, a court cannot pass a community sentence unless the offence(s) is sufficiently serious to justify such a sentence, and any restriction on liberty involved must be commensurate with the seriousness of the offence (again emphasising the principle of proportionality). S.147 creates a new *generic community order* that can consist of a combination of the different requirements (*e.g.* unpaid work, curfew, drug and/ or alcohol rehabilitation) specified in s.177. The combination of requirements must be those most suitable for the particular offender.

What are the rules on fines?

Under CJA, s.164, the amount of a fine must reflect *both* the seriousness of the offence *and* the offender's ability to pay, again emphasising the proportionality.

What other sentences are available?

There are a number of miscellaneous sanctions available to the court. Where the offence is not sufficiently serious to justify a community sentence or a fine, then the court can pass a **conditional or absolute discharge**. The court may also impose a **compensation order, confiscation order,** or **drug treatment and testing order**.

What are the special sentences for young offenders?

Special sentences apply to young offenders (under 18) with an emphasis on reform, rehabilitation and welfare. There are a number of pre-court orders available, designed to address minor criminality or anti-social behaviour outside the criminal justice system—acceptable behaviour contracts, anti-social behaviour orders, local child curfews, and child safety orders. For first and second minor offences, the police can also use a system of **reprimands** and **final warnings**. The only custodial sentence for young offenders between 12 and 17 is a **detention and training order** (for between four months and two years). The second half of the sentence is a period of community supervision by a Youth Offending Team. This sentence is reserved for the most serious and/or persistent young offenders. Various community sentences are also available, including **curfew orders, attendance centre orders, action plan orders,** and **supervision orders**. The court can also impose a **parenting order** on the parents/carers of a young offender.

How effective is the system in achieving its aims?

Overall, only approximately 20 per cent of reported crimes result in a conviction. This is known as the 'justice gap' and means that 80 per cent of crimes go unpunished, significantly weakening the deterrent effect of the system and damaging public confidence. Also, custodial sentences are noticeably ineffective in preventing re-offending. Of prisoners released in 1997, 58 per cent were reconvicted within two years (the reconviction rate for 18–20 year old male prisoners was 72 per cent). This is due to prison overcrowding (described by Lord Woolf, the Lord Chief Justice, as a "cancer eating at the ability of the prison service to deliver") and consequent lack of effective rehabilitation programmes. The lack of effective rehabilitation programmes highlights the link between offending and social exclusion. Offenders are far more likely than non-offenders to have a poor education and employment record, to have experienced family breakdown and housing problems, and to have drug, alcohol or mental health problems. For example, many prisoners' basic skills are very poor. 80 per cent have the writing skills, 65 per cent the numeracy skills and 50 per cent the reading skills at or below the level of an 11-year-old child. As the Social Exclusion Unit has stated, there is a considerable risk that a prison sentence might actually make the factors associated with re-offending worse. For example, a third lose their house while in prison, two-thirds lose their job, over a fifth face increased financial problems and over two-fifths lose contact with their family. There are also real dangers of mental and physical health deteriorating further, of life and thinking skills being eroded, and of prisoners being introduced to drugs. By aggravating the factors associated with re-offending, prison sentences can prove counter-productive as a contribution to crime reduction and public safety. This is particularly so in relation to short prison sentences, although it is hoped that the new "Custody Plus" and "Intermittent Custody" sentences will improve this situation.

9. CIVIL PROCESS

What options are available for someone involved in a civil dispute?

There are *four* main options:

(1) **Negotiation**—the disputing parties can negotiate a mutually acceptable settlement.

(2) **Mediation/Conciliation**—a third party can be used to help the disputing parties negotiate a mutually acceptable settlement (known as "**assisted settlement**")

(3) **Arbitration**—the disputing parties can agree to use a third party (often a member of the Chartered Institute of Arbitrators) to decide on a settlement (known as "**alternative adjudication**").

(4) **Litigation**—the disputing parties can take their dispute to court for resolution.

The first two options are sometimes referred to as "win-win" approaches, while the second two are sometimes referred to as 'win-lose' approaches.

What are the civil courts?

Court	Jurisdiction
House of Lords	Civil (and criminal) appeals that raise a point of law of general public importance.
Court of Appeal (Civil Division)	Civil appeals.
Divisional Courts	• Queen's Bench—judicial review. • Chancery—taxation and land registration appeals. • Family—appeals on family matters from the magistrates' court.
High Court	• Queen's Bench—high value claims in contract and tort. • Chancery—land, trusts, contentious probate, company, partnership and bankruptcy matters, intellectual property. • Family—matrimonial and family matters (including defended divorce), non-contentious probate.
Crown Court	• Licensing appeals from the magistrates' court.
County Court	• Smaller value claims in contract and tort. • Undefended divorce.
Magistrates' Court	• Minor family matters. • Some forms of statutory debt (*e.g.* non-payment of Council Tax). • Licensing (*e.g.* liquor licenses).

How does the "Three-Track" system work?

Before issuing a civil claim, the claimant must follow a *pre-action protocol*, intended to encourage early settlement (as there may be serious costs consequences for any party who unreasonably refuses an offer to settle) and/or use of ADR. Where no early settlement takes place, the claimant must issue a *claim form*. Claims for less than £15,000 (£50,000 in personal injury claims) are issued in the County Court. Higher value claims are issued in the High Court (although straightforward cases can be transferred to the County Court). Within 14 days the defendant must either: (a) admit the claim; (b) file a defence; (c) acknowledge service (giving another 14 days to file a defence). If the claim is defended, both parties must complete an *allocation questionnaire*, after which the procedural judge will allocate the case to one of the three 'tracks':

(1) **Small Claims Track**—this is an informal process before a District Judge in the County Court. All claims of less than £5,000 (£1,000 in personal injury) are automatically referred to this track. Higher value claims can use this track if both parties and the procedural judge agree. The idea is that parties are able to represent themselves, and there are rules on costs to discourage professional representation.

(2) **Fast Track**—this is for claims between £5,000 and £15,000 (£1,000 and £15,000 in personal injury) and where the trial is not expected to last more than one day (five hours). A timetable is set towards a trial within 30 weeks, and strict rules on costs and the use of expert witnesses are designed to encourage efficient presentation and settlement.

(3) **Multi-Track**—this is for claims above £15,000 and lower value claims of unusual complexity. The judge acts as a trial manager, chairing a case management conference to establish a timetable, monitoring progress, and holding a pre-trial review to explore settlement possibilities and, if necessary, set a trial agenda.

What were the "Woolf reforms" to civil justice?

Following concerns over costs and delays in the civil justice system, Lord Woolf proposed a series of major reforms, with an "overriding objective" of justice, efficiency, and proportionality, in his 1996 report 'Access to Justice'. These reforms were implemented in 1999. The main reforms were:

(1) The introduction of the "three-track" system.
(2) The introduction of a single set of Civil Procedure Rules.
(3) The encouragement of early settlements and the use of alternative dispute resolution (ADR—*e.g.* mediation, arbitration).
(4) More effective case management by judges.
(5) Modernised terminology (*e.g.* "plaintiff" became "claimant", and "writ" became "claim form").

The **anticipated benefits** were:

(1) Less civil litigation.
(2) Litigation would be less adversarial, more co-operative, and less complex.

(3) Fewer delays.
(4) Costs would be more affordable and more proportionate to the value and complexity of individual cases.
(5) Resources would be more efficiently deployed.

How effective have the "Woolf reforms" been?

The Department for Constitutional Affairs has conducted two reviews of the 'Woolf reforms'. These indicate that the reforms have been largely successful in achieving their aims:

(1) There has been a fall in the number of civil claims.
(2) Pre-action protocols are working well to encourage early settlement and a more co-operative culture.
(3) In addition to a rise in early settlements, there has been an increase in the use of ADR.
(4) The use of single joint experts has worked well, contributing to a less adversarial culture and promoting early settlement.
(5) Case management conferences are working well and delays have been reduced.

There remain, however, some areas of concern:

(1) The position on costs is unclear with statistics difficult to obtain and conflicting anecdotal evidence. It may be that some lawyers are 'front-loading' costs onto the pre-trial phase.
(2) There have been delays in introducing the necessary information technology into the courts.
(3) Enforcement proceedings remain complex and time-consuming.

---

10. ALTERNATIVE DISPUTE RESOLUTION

What is "ADR"?

ADR refers to the range of mechanisms available for resolving civil disputes without going to court. Historically, civil litigation has been expensive, time-consuming, often disproportionate to the value of the claim, and its adversarial nature is sometimes inappropriate and unhelpful (*e.g.* in family disputes, especially involving children). While the "Woolf reforms" (see previous chapter) have gone a long way to reducing these problems, ADR remains a vital part of civil dispute resolution—indeed, "Woolf" was intended to increase early settlement and the use of ADR. ADR embraces a range of mechanisms, from the very informal, such as mediation, through more formal options, such as arbitration, to the most formal, tribunals.

How does the tribunal system work?

There are a large number of administrative (public) tribunals dealing with a wide range of disputes arising from statutory systems of administration (*e.g.* Mental Health Review Tribunals, Employment Tribunals, Social Security Tribunals, etc.). A tribunal will usually have three members (a legally-qualified chair and two lay experts). Appeal on a point of law is generally possible to the High Court. Tribunals are also subject to the supervisory jurisdiction of the Queen's Bench Divisional Court, and are monitored by the Council on Tribunals. This is all to ensure the legal accuracy and procedural fairness of tribunal decisions and proceedings. There are also a number of domestic (private) tribunals, largely concerned with the discipline of members of a particular profession (*e.g.* doctors).

The main **advantages** of tribunals are:

- ☑ Proceedings are **inexpensive**, both in absolute terms and relative to the cost of litigation.
- ☑ Proceedings are **quicker** than litigation, allowing tribunals to deal with over 1 million cases per year.
- ☑ Proceedings are kept as **informal** as possible, making them more accessible than formal litigation.
- ☑ Lay members are appointed for their **expertise** in the subject-matter of the tribunal.

However, in 2001, the Leggatt Review of Tribunals, while acknowledging the huge contribution made by tribunals to administrative justice, did criticise the system for its complex, uncoordinated nature that posed problems for users. The review recommended a unified Tribunals Service to ensure consistency, a more logical structure, simplified procedures, better training, and clearer guidance for users, to ensure a system that was informal, simple, efficient, proportionate, and user-friendly. The relationship of these proposals to the "Woolf reforms" is obvious, and the Government intends to implement the main proposals by 2008.

How does arbitration work?

Arbitration is the reference of a dispute to a third party (often a member of the Chartered Institute of Arbitrators) for a decision. While essentially a private arrangement, arbitration is subject to the supervisory jurisdiction of the courts and regulated by statute, again to ensure justice and fairness. Arbitration is commonly used to resolve **commercial disputes** (many commercial contracts contain an arbitration clause), **industrial disputes** (through the intervention of the Advisory Conciliation and Arbitration Service—ACAS), and **consumer disputes** (many trade associations—*e.g.* Association of British Travel Agents (ABTA)— offer an arbitration service). In addition to sharing the advantages of tribunals, arbitration has the additional advantages of:

- ☑ **Privacy**—arbitration is a private arrangement, enabling sensitive commercial information to remain confidential.
- ☑ **Convenience**—the hearing takes place at a time and venue convenient to the parties.

How does mediation and conciliation work?

Mediation and conciliation are essentially less formal versions of arbitration—**"assisted settlement"** rather than **"alternative adjudication"**. Rather than make the decision, the role of the mediator or conciliator is to assist the disputing parties in reaching a mutually agreed settlement. The parties may also be able to negotiate a mutually acceptable settlement between them, without the need for any third party intervention. As both parties have a role in determining the solution, negotiation, mediation, and conciliation are sometimes referred to as "win-win" options, as contrasted with the "win-lose" approach of arbitration, tribunals, and litigation. This is an obvious advantage where the parties have an on-going relationship (*e.g.* neighbours, business partners, etc.).

11. THE LEGAL PROFESSION

What do barristers do and how are they trained?

There are approximately 10,300 practising barristers in England and Wales. Barristers are specialist legal advisors and courtroom advocates. As such, they not only spend time representing clients in court, but also work on pre-trial preparation, giving "opinions" (a considered view of the merits of a case or on a point of law), and meeting with solicitors and clients. The governing body for barristers is the Bar Council, with responsibility for education, regulation (of professional standards and complaints), and representation (of the interests of the Bar as a whole).

The education and training of barristers falls into *three* stages:

(1) **Academic stage**—either a law degree, or a non-law degree followed by a one-year conversion course (the Common Professional Examination—CPE).

(2) **Vocational Stage**—a one-year vocational course with an emphasis on skills and procedure (the Bar Vocational Course—BVC).

(3) **Practical stage**—a one-year period of practical training (known as "pupillage") with an experienced barrister.

The trainee must also join one of the four Inns of Court. After qualification, a barrister must obtain a place in Chambers from which to practice—although barristers are self-employed, they do share sets of offices (known as Chambers) where they share running costs and the services of a Clerk and other support staff. During their first three years' practice, a barrister must complete the New Practitioners Programme, and thereafter undertake Continuing Professional Development (CPD) to update their knowledge and skills.

What is the QC system and is it necessary?

Around 10 per cent of barristers are appointed to the rank of Queen's Counsel (QC or "silk") by the Queen on the advice of the Lord Chancellor. For the barrister, becoming a QC enables them to charge higher fees and offers an increased chance of judicial appointment. It is also supposed to indicate the most experienced and able barristers (a quality mark) and provide a career structure. However, many organisations, such as the Law Society and Office of Fair Trading, are highly critical of the QC system:

- ☒ Dividing the profession into an elite 10 per cent and an undifferentiated rump of 90 per cent hardly provides an effective career structure.
- ☒ QC status is not a reliable quality mark, as no additional qualifications or assessment are required, and there is no mechanism for subsequent review or for the award to be rescinded.
- ☒ The QC system distorts competition and artificially raises the cost of legal services.

In 2003, the Department for Constitutional Affairs published a consultation paper on the future of Queen's Counsel, seeking views on various options including reform or abolition.

What do solicitors do and how are they trained?

There are approximately 89,000 practising solicitors in England and Wales (with around 80 per cent in private practice). Solicitors are general legal advisors. Typically around 80 per cent of their work involves conveyancing, commercial, matrimonial, and probate matters, although solicitors in the large 'City' firms may well specialise in other areas (*e.g.* intellectual property, mergers, or media law). Solicitors may also represent their clients in court—almost all advocacy in the magistrates' court is undertaken by solicitors, and, since 1993, solicitors with appropriate qualifications and experience have been able to appear in the higher courts, although relatively few choose to do so, preferring to instruct a barrister. The governing body for solicitors is the Law Society, with responsibility for education, regulation (of professional standards and complaints), and representation (of the interests of solicitors as a whole).

The education and training of solicitors falls into *three* stages:

(1) **Academic stage**—either a law degree, or a non-law degree followed by a one-year conversion course (the Common Professional Examination—CPE).
(2) **Vocational Stage**—a one-year vocational course with an emphasis on skills (the Legal Practice Course—LPC).

(3) **Practical stage**—a two-year training contract (formerly
known as articles) with an experienced solicitor. During
this time they must also complete the Professional Skills
Course.

There is also the so-called **"learn-as-you-earn" route**, where
someone working in a legal environment can study and qualify
as a Legal Executive and then, if they wish, go on to qualify as a
solicitor. After qualification, a solicitor must undertake Continuing Professional Development (CPD) to update their knowledge
and skills. Most will obtain employment in an existing practice
as an assistant solicitor, although some work in other parts of
the private sector or in central or local government.

What do paralegals do and how are they trained?

Paralegals are persons with formal legal training but who are
not fully qualified as either solicitors or barristers. The best
known are Legal Executives, who perform professional work in
specialised areas. Their governing body is the Institute of Legal
Executives. A more recent type of paralegal is the Licensed
Coveyancer, established in 1987, when solicitors lost their mono-
poly over conveyancing (the legal side of buying and selling
land). While many are self employed, some work for banks,
lenders, and property developers. Their governing body is the
Council for Licensed Conveyancers.

What is the role of the Crown Prosecution Service?

The Crown Prosecution Service (CPS), headed by the Director of
Public Prosecutions, was established under the Prosecution of
Offenders Act 1985. Following charge, it is the CPS that is
responsible for the conduct of criminal prosecutions. In deciding
whether a prosecution should continue, the case must satisfy the
two tests in the Code for Crown Prosecutors:

(1) **Evidential sufficiency**—there must be sufficient reliable
and admissible evidence to give rise to a realistic prospect
of conviction.
(2) **Public interest**—the prosecution must be in the public
interest. Relevant factors stated in the Code include the
likely penalty, any discriminatory motive for the offence,
the age and mental health of the offender, and the attitude
of the victim.

Are there any problems faced by women and ethnic minorities in pursuing a legal career?

Historically, the legal profession has been white, male, and middle-class, with both women and ethic minorities being significantly under-represented. In recent years, the situation has improved somewhat:

- ☑ Over one-third of solicitors currently practising are women.
- ☑ Over 50 per cent of newly-qualified solicitors are women.
- ☑ Approximately 15 per cent of newly-qualified solicitors are from the ethnic minorities.

However, a number of significant problems remain:

- ☒ Women face significant pay discrimination. A 2003 survey found that experienced women solicitors tend to earn around 15 per cent less than their male counterparts.
- ☒ Women still face a "glass ceiling", barring access to senior positions within the profession.
- ☒ Ethnic minority applicants have significantly more difficulty obtaining pupillage and training places than their white counterparts. This is partly because many ethic minority students attend the "new" universities which are less favoured by the profession.
- ☒ A 2002 Inns of Court inquiry found evidence of "systematic ethnic bias" at the Bar (*e.g.* while 60 per cent of white applicants were successful in applying for training funds, only 26 per cent of ethnic minority applicants were successful).
- ☒ Some measures intended to improve access have had unexpected negative effects (*e.g.* the introduction of a £10,000 minimum wage for pupil barristers has resulted in a significant decline in the number of pupillages available).
- ☒ The progress of recent years is threatened by the introduction of tuition and top-up fees for degree students. The fact that a law student may finish their academic and vocational training with debts of around £25,000 may well deter students from poorer backgrounds from pursuing a legal career.

Does it make sense to have a formal distinction between solicitors and barristers?

In the past, the formal division of the profession has been a controversial issue. While some have argued for "fusion" into a single profession, both the Royal Commission on Legal Services (Benson Commission) (1979), and the Marre Committee (1988) recommended retaining the division. However, partly as a result of changes made by the Courts and Legal Services Act 1990 and the Access to Justice Act 1999, the 'fusion debate' is far less significant today:

(1) Many of the restrictive practices associated with the division have been abolished (*e.g.* solicitors can now enjoy rights of audience in all courts, and some groups, such as accountants and architects, can approach barristers directly).

(2) Studies have shown that any 'double-manning' that arises in a case from employing both a solicitor and barrister accounts for only a small proportion of the total costs of legal services. Therefore, any cost savings arising from fusion are likely to be minimal.

(3) There seems to be a natural division of labour between office lawyers and trial lawyers (or litigators), both from the evidence of jurisdictions (*e.g.* USA) where there is no formal division, and from the fact that relatively few solicitors have taken up extended advocacy rights, still preferring to use a barrister as a specialist advocate.

Nevertheless, a 2001 report by the Office of Fair Trading continued to criticise the structure of the profession as anti-competitive and against the interests of consumers.

Is the profession adequately accountable to the public for the quality of its services?

Despite the abolition of the "advocate's immunity" from liability for negligent advocacy (when the House of Lords used the 1966 Practice Statement in *Arthur JS Hall v Simons* [2000] to depart from their previous decision in *Rondel v Worsley* [1967]), significant concerns remain that a self-regulating profession is not sufficiently accountable to the consumer for the quality of the service it provides:

☒ The work of the Office for the Supervision of Solicitors in investigating professional misconduct and inadequate professional services has been repeatedly criticised as inadequate by the Legal Services Ombudsman (who investigates complaints about the way in which the Law Society and Bar Council deal with complaints from clients). In April 2004, the OSS was replaced by the Law Society's Consumer Complaints Service. The CSS investigates complaints about poor service and overcharging. Complaints about professional misconduct are referred to the Law Society's Compliance Directorate.

☒ A recent survey for the Bar Council found that 74 per cent of clients were very dissatisfied with the handling of their complaints (only 3 per cent of barristers complained against were equally dissatisfied).

In 2003, the Government established the Clementi Review of the Legal Profession to examine both the provision and regulation of legal services. The Lord Chancellor, Lord Falconer, has said that there is a "significant chance" that, following the review, a fully independent regulatory system will replace the present system of self-regulation.

12. THE JUDICIARY

What do judges do?

In both civil and criminal trials, the judge is responsible for the fair conduct of the trial, and decides any questions of law or procedure that arise. In most civil cases (as civil juries are rare), the judge also decides questions of fact, reaches a verdict, and, where appropriate, decides on a remedy. Following the "Woolf" reforms, the judge also takes an active role as a case/trial manager in civil cases, and is also expected to perform a similar role in criminal cases (*R v Jisl* [2004]). In serious criminal trials, the judge sums up the evidence to the jury and directs them on the relevant law. Following conviction, it is the judge that determines sentence. Judges (especially those in the appellate courts) also have an important law-making role, both in the creation and development of precedent, and in the interpretation and application of legislation.

How are judges appointed and trained?

The qualifications required, and appointment process for, the different types of judge are:

Judge	Qualifications	Appointment	Process
Lord of Appeal in Ordinary (Law Lord)	Generally appointed from among the experienced judges of the Court of Appeal.	By The Queen on the recommendation of the Prime Minister, advised by the Lord Chancellor.	By invitation.
Lord Justice of Appeal	10 year High Court qualification or High Court judge.	By The Queen on the recommendation of the Prime Minister, advised by the Lord Chancellor.	By invitation.
High Court Judge	10 year High Court qualification or min. two years experience as a Circuit Judge.	By The Queen on the recommendation of the Lord Chancellor.	By invitation or application (no interview).
Circuit Judge	10 year Crown Court or County Court qualification or Recorder.	By The Queen on the recommendation of the Lord Chancellor.	Application and interview.
Recorder	10 year Crown Court or 10 year County Court qualification.	By The Queen on the recommendation of the Lord Chancellor.	Application and interview.
District Judge	Seven year general qualification.	By the Lord Chancellor.	Application and interview.
District Judge (Magistrates' Court)	Seven year general qualification.	By The Queen on the recommendation of the Lord Chancellor.	Application and interview.

The training for new judges is the responsibility of the Judicial Studies Board, and consists of a one-week residential course on procedure, sentencing, and issues such as racial awareness, followed by at least one week sitting alongside an experienced judge. Thereafter, judges attend refresher courses and seminars on new legislation.

Judges hold office 'during good behaviour'. High Court judges and above can only be removed for a breach of this obligation or by an address in both Houses of Parliament. The Lord Chancellor can dismiss Circuit Judges, Recorders, and District Judges for incapacity or misbehaviour. Judges retire at age 70.

What are the senior judicial posts?

The head of the judiciary is the Lord Chancellor, appointed by The Queen on the advice of the Prime Minister. The Lord Chancellor, in addition to being head of the judiciary and effectively responsible for most judicial appointments, is also a senior member of the Government (with responsibility for the administration of justice), and Speaker of the House of Lords. This triple role, as part of the Judiciary, Executive, and Legislature, is a clear breach of the separation of powers. There have been increasing calls to reform or abolish the role of Lord Chancellor (*e.g.* by the law reform group 'Justice', and by Professor Diana Woodhouse). Also, a 2003 report for the Council of Europe argued that this triple role contravened the European Convention on Human Rights (in particular, the right under Article 6 to a fair trial before an independent and impartial tribunal). In response to these concerns, and following a consultation exercise, the Constitutional Reform Bill 2004 proposed radical reforms:

(1) The abolition of the office of Lord Chancellor.
(2) The Lord Chief Justice to be head of the judiciary.
(3) Executive responsibility for the administration of justice to be given to a Secretary of State for Constitutional Affairs.
(4) A new Supreme Court to replace the Judicial Committee of the House of Lords.
(5) A new process for appointing judges (see below).

However, the Bill has proved highly controversial and it remains to be seen what the final shape of reform will be.

The other senior judicial positions are:

Post	Presides over. . .	Qualifications	Appointment
Lord Chief Justice	Court of Appeal (Criminal Division) and Queen's Bench Division of the High Court.	10 year High Court qualification, or High Court judge, or Lord Justice of Appeal.	By The Queen on the recommendation of the Prime Minister, advised by the Lord Chancellor.
Master of the Rolls	Court of Appeal (Civil Division).		
Vice-Chancellor	Chancery Division of the High Court.		
President of the Family Division	Family Division of the High Court.		

Should the procedure for appointing judges be reformed?

The present system, whereby most judicial appointments are made by the Lord Chancellor (himself a political appointment), has been subject to a number of significant criticisms:

(1) **The process is too informal and secretive**. The Commissioner for Judicial Appointments (established in 2002) has criticised the present system of "secret soundings" for allowing scope for decisions to be influenced by anecdote, gossip, and prejudice.

(2) **It results in an unrepresentative judiciary**. Statistics for 2002 showed that 67 per cent of judges had been educated at public school. Furthermore, only 9 per cent of judges are women, and only 1 per cent from the ethnic minorities. Again, the Commissioner for Judicial Appointments has criticised the system for producing a judiciary that is "overwhelmingly white, male, and from a narrow social and educational background", and for a "systemic bias. . . that affects the position of women [and] ethnic minority candidates. . . in relation to. . . judicial appointments".

In response to these criticisms, and following a consultation exercise, the Constitutional Reform Bill 2004 proposed a new system of judicial appointments. Candidates would be selected by a Judicial Appointments Commission (consisting of judges, lawyers, and lay members) and then recommended to the Secretary of State for Constitutional Affairs. The Secretary of State could only reject one candidate—following rejection, he would have to appoint/recommend the appointment of either the new or original nominee. However, as noted above, the Bill has proved controversial, and some people still believe the Commission should be an 'appointing' rather than a 'recommending' body, and that there should be no political involvement by the Secretary of State.

What does "judicial independence" mean and why is it important?

"Judicial independence" means that judges should be free from pressure or influence by the Executive, interest groups, and litigants. It is important because it is a pre-condition of impartiality and, therefore, of a fair trial, as required under Article 6 of the European Convention on Human Rights. Formal judicial independence is guaranteed in a number of ways (although concerns remain over political involvement in the appointment of judges, despite the inclusion of a statutory guarantee of judicial independence in the Constitutional Reform Bill 2004— see above):

(1) Judicial salaries/pensions are set by an independent review body.
(2) Judges cannot carry on any other business or profession, or hold any other paid appointment.
(3) Judges should disqualify themselves from any case where they might/might appear to be biased (see the problems caused by Lord Hoffmann's participation in the Pinochet case in 1998), or in which they have a personal interest (*e.g.* as a shareholder in a litigant company).

The informal independence of the judiciary from other parts of the 'Establishment' has been doubted by some (*e.g.* Professor John Griffith), arguing that because of their social and educational background (see above), judges tend to be conservative in outlook. However, others (notably Lord Denning) have argued that the judges are perfectly capable of standing up to the Executive and protecting the rights of the individual, and recent conflicts between the judiciary and the Government (especially the Home Secretary) seem to indicate that this view is correct.

13. MAGISTRATES AND JURIES

What are "lay magistrates" and how are they appointed and trained?

Lay magistrates are ordinary men and women with no formal legal qualifications, who sit and decide cases in the magistrates' courts (with advice available from a legally-qualified clerk). They are part-time, unpaid, amateur judges (although they do receive some financial allowances). The first magistrates (or Justices of the Peace) were appointed in 1195, although they did not assume a judicial role until the 14th Century. There are currently around 30,000 lay magistrates, generally sitting as a bench of three magistrates, exercising both civil and criminal jurisdiction:

(1) **Civil**—minor family matters (sitting as a specially-trained mixed bench in a Family Proceedings Court), some categories of civil debt (*e.g.* non-payment of Council Tax), and some licensing matters (*e.g.* liquor licences).

(2) **Criminal**—Early Administrative Hearings for all criminal cases (deciding applications for bail and legal aid, ordering reports, and sending those charged with indictable offences for trial at the Crown Court), Mode of Trial hearings for those charged with "either-way" offences, and summary trials for those charged with summary offences (or "either-way" being tried summarily). Magistrates' sentencing powers are limited to 12 months (Criminal Justice Act 2003, s.164), although they can commit someone for sentence at the Crown Court if they believe their powers to be inadequate. Magistrates also sit alongside a judge in the Crown Court to hear appeals against conviction or sentence. When dealing with young offenders (aged 10–17), specially-trained magistrates sit as a mixed bench in a Youth Court—see Chapter 7).

There are no formal qualifications required to be a magistrate (though some people are disqualified—*e.g.* undischarged bankrupts, serving police officers). To be appointed, candidates must have the 'magisterial qualities' of good character, personal integrity, common sense, sound judgement, and good knowledge of the local community. Magistrates are appointed by the Lord Chancellor on advice from a Local Advisory Committee (consisting largely of serving and retired magistrates). In considering applicants, the Committee must take into account the "Bench requirements" (*i.e.* that the bench should broadly reflect the community it serves in terms of gender, ethnic origin, geographical spread, occupation and political affiliation). This reflects the magisterial ideal of "local justice by local people".

While lay magistrates are amateur judges, since 1966 they have received some formal training. This now takes the form of the Magistrates National Training Initiative (MNTI or "Minty"), a mentoring system whereby experienced magistrates help new magistrates achieve competencies in jurisdiction, basic law and procedure, judicial reasoning and conduct, and teamwork. As noted above, magistrates may also receive special training to sit on a Family or Youth bench.

What are the advantages and disadvantages of lay magistrates?

The lay magistracy is extremely important as it deals with approximately 95 per cent of all criminal cases, and almost all cases concerning young offenders. Therefore, there must be very good reasons for trusting such an important task to ordinary lay people.

The **advantages** of the lay magistracy are:

- ☑ They bring the **values and common sense of ordinary people** to the legal system, preventing it becoming the preserve of a legal elite and remote from the concerns of ordinary people.
- ☑ By using people who live and/or work locally, the magistracy should **reflect the concerns of the local community**.
- ☑ Using unpaid lay magistrates helps to **keep down the cost** of the criminal justice system. However, comparisons of costs per disposal between lay magistrates and District Judges reveal less of a saving than might be expected.

The **disadvantages** are:

☒ Contrary to the ideal, the lay magistracy is **not representative** of society at large. The Advisory Committee system, together with financial and employment constraints, produce a magistracy that is largely white, middle-aged, and middle-class. Regarding political affiliation, a 2003 survey by the Department for Constitutional Affairs (DCA) found that 35 per cent of magistrates regarded themselves as Conservatives, 25 per cent Labour, 13 per cent Liberal Democrats, with 20 per cent uncommitted. To seek to improve the social and racial mix of the magistracy, in 2003 the DCA launched a National Recruitment Strategy for magistrates, including a £4 million campaign aimed at recruiting younger magistrates and more candidates from the ethnic minorities and working-class. Also, a Magistrates Shadowing Scheme, in partnership with Operation Black Vote, has increased the proportion of new magistrates from the ethnic minorities from 5 per cent in 1994 to 9.3 per cent in 2001. Nevertheless, continued efforts are needed to ensure the magistracy more accurately reflects the community it serves, essential to its continued legitimacy.

☒ Due to their social background, many **magistrates** are said to be **prosecution and conviction-minded**, to the detriment of defendants.

☒ Studies have shown considerable **inconsistencies in sentencing** between benches. If magistrates are to reflect local concerns, some inconsistency is inevitable. Nevertheless, the present inconsistencies are beyond anything that could be accounted for by this reason alone. For example, 2001 Home Office Statistics showed that magistrates in Southeast Northumberland gave an absolute or conditional discharge in 46 per cent of cases, against a national average of 21 per cent, and only 10 per cent in Havering, East London.

What is the role of the jury in a criminal trial and how are jurors selected?

A criminal jury has twelve members, and its role is to decide questions of fact and reach a verdict. In order to convict a defendant, the jury must be satisfied of his guilt beyond a reasonable doubt. They receive no training, but are shown a short video that explains how they were selected, their role in the trial, and what to expect in court.

Under the Juries Act 1974 (as amended by the Criminal Justice Act 2003), anyone aged between 18 and 70, who has been a UK resident for at least five years, and is on the electoral register is eligible for jury service. Selection for service by the Jury Central Summoning Bureau is random. People with a mental illness are ineligible for service, while those with a significant criminal record are disqualified. A serving member of the armed services can be excused if this is requested by their commanding officer. Anyone else must serve if summonsed unless they can show compelling reasons why their service should be deferred or (if they cannot serve within 12 months) excused. Reasons for deferral could include ill health, religious festivals, care responsibilities, pre-booked holidays, or examinations. Reasons for excusal could include chronic ill-health, long-term care responsibilities, insufficient understanding of English, or membership of a religious order whose beliefs are incompatible with jury service.

The jury must try to reach a unanimous verdict. After a minimum of two hours' discussion, the judge may accept a majority verdict (of 11–1 or 10–2). If the jury cannot reach a verdict, the case is discharged and may be re-tried with a different jury.

What are the advantages and disadvantages of juries?

While the Contempt of Court Act 1981 prevents research on the workings of juries, and the House of Lords recently upheld the prohibition on investigating what happens in the jury room (*R v Mirza* [2004]), the **advantages** claimed for trial by jury are:

☑ The **symbolic value** of community participation in serious criminal trials.

☑ The **right of the jury to return a verdict according to its conscience** (established in *Bushell's Case* [1670]) allows the jury to acquit in the face of the evidence where they believe a particular law or prosecution to be unjust (sometimes referred to as a "perverse" verdict)—*e.g. R v Ponting* [1985], *R v Pottle and Randle* [1990], *R v Melchett and others* [2000].

☑ This also means the jury can act as a **safeguard against state oppression**—Lord Devlin famously described the jury as the "lamp that shows that freedom lives".

☑ The use of the jury **spreads the burden** of deciding guilt or innocence, rather than it falling on a single judge.

The **disadvantages** are said to be:

☒ Juries are **open to intimidation**. This led to the removal of jury trial in Northern Ireland for terrorist offences (tried by a judge alone in a "Diplock" court). The Metropolitan Police regard jury 'tampering' as a major obstacle to dealing with organised crime, and spend an average of £4.5 million per year on jury protection. As a consequence, the Criminal Justice Act 2003, s.44, allows for trial by judge alone where there is a 'real and present danger' of jury tampering.

☒ Juries **cannot understand complex evidence**, especially in complex fraud trials. The Roskill Committee (1986) proposed the use of a judge with two lay assessors in such cases. The CJA 2003, s.43, provides for a trial by judge alone in fraud trials where the length and/or complexity of the trial would make the trial excessively burdensome for a jury. Because of its controversial nature, this provision will only come into force following the consent of Parliament to a commencement order through the affirmative resolution procedure.

☒ Juries do **not have to give reasons** for their verdict (famously, one jury was found to have used a ouija board), whereas a judge alone must give reasons.

☒ Juries are **susceptible to persuasion**, and may be swayed by clever, persuasive, or forceful advocacy rather than by the evidence.

☒ Jurors may bring **prejudices** into the jury room.

☒ Juries are **unrepresentative**. Until recently, many people were able to use the categories of excusal under the Juries Act 1974 to avoid service—in 2001, almost one-third of those summonsed were excused. The reforms made by the CJA 2003 should make it far more difficult for people to avoid service.

14. ACCESS TO LEGAL SERVICES

Why is access to legal services an important issue?

A 2001 report by the Social Exclusion Unit (*"Legal and Advice Services: A pathway out of social exclusion"*) stated "legal rights are useless if people do not know what those rights are or do not know how to enforce them, and they are unable to receive expert independent help", and that "lack of access to reliable legal advice can be a contributing factor in creating and maintaining social exclusion".

What does the "unmet need for legal services" mean?

Academic research in the 1970s identified *three* forms of unmet need:

(1) Where someone does not recognise their problem as being a legal one.
(2) Where the problem is recognised as being legal, but the person is unable for a variety of reasons to access the services available.
(3) Where the problem is recognised as being legal, but no developed service exists to provide the appropriate help.

What causes the unmet need?

There are *four* main factors:

(1) **Geographical**—the uneven distribution of solicitors and firms across the country can make it difficult for people in some areas to access services locally. 2002 Law Society statistics show that Greater London has 26 per cent of all firms and 42 per cent of all solicitors with only 13.8 per cent of the population, whereas the South West has 9.5 per cent of the population with only 8.7 per cent of firms and 7.9 per cent of solicitors.
(2) **Psychological**—many people, particularly from the least advantaged sections of the community, can feel intimidated by the prospect of consulting a solicitor and getting involved with the law.
(3) **Knowledge**—the emphasis of legal education and training on areas of law relevant to the profession's traditional client base—essentially property and commercial

matters—can make it difficult to find a solicitor with relevant expertise in other, less profitable areas.

(4) **Cost**—the cost of private legal services is quite simply beyond the means of many people and a considerable deterrent to many more.

Apart from the legal profession, where can someone get legal advice?

Other sources of advice include:

(1) **Local authority advice units**, typically covering housing, benefit and consumer issues.
(2) Many **charities** offer advice on issues relating to their area of work.
(3) **Trade unions** offer advice to members on employment law issues, and increasingly offer a range of other services.
(4) The **motoring organisations**—both the AA and RAC offer advice to their members.
(5) Both the **broadcast and print media** can offer general advice through, for example, phone-ins and advice columns.
(6) The major contribution comes from **not-for-profit providers** such as Citizens Advice Bureaux and Law Centres. There are approximately 2,000 CAB, frequently located in high streets and other accessible locations. They deal with approximately six million enquiries per year, of which around one-third involve legal issues. Given their geographical distribution, informal atmosphere, specialist knowledge of issues such as welfare, and the fact their advice is free, CAB address all the factors giving rise to the unmet need, and have a key role to play in any successful strategy to resolve it. The Benson Commission in 1979 viewed CAB as excellently placed to provide a preliminary advice and referral service. However, historically they have not received the funding necessary. There are approximately 50 Law Centres, located in London and other major metropolitan areas. They share the advantages of CAB, with the additional benefit of being specifically concerned with legal issues. Their work was similarly praised by the Benson Commission, and could make a major impact, alongside CAB, in any co-ordinated

approach to resolving the unmet need. However, inadequate and insecure funding has limited their ability to do so.

Apart from private finance, how else can legal services be funded?

Alternative sources of funding include:

(1) **Private insurance**—around 33 million people (over half of all British households) have some form of legal insurance.
(2) *Pro bono* **work**—the profession (through the Free Representation Unit, the Bar Pro Bono Unit, and the Solicitors Pro Bono Group) is increasingly concerned to establish *pro bono* work—providing some services free of charge—as an important aspect of lawyers' duties.
(3) **Conditional fees**—the Courts and Legal Services Act 1990 enabled lawyers to enter into conditional fee arrangements for a limited range of cases, where the lawyer takes a reduced fee or even no fee if they lose the case (hence 'no-win, no-fee'), but can charge an additional 'success fee' if they win. The only financial cost to the claimant at the outset of the case is the insurance policy to cover the other side's costs should they lose. The main argument against such arrangements was that it was undesirable for a lawyer to have a direct financial interest in the outcome of a case. The main arguments in favour were that they would relieve the burden on legal aid, and also widen access to justice by addressing the "middle income trap" (see below).

What were the problems with Legal Aid system?

The Legal Aid system (providing state subsidies for private legal services) was introduced in 1949. For the following 50 years (together with the Green Form Scheme, established in 1972, and ABWOR—assistance by way of representation—established in 1979), this was the main strategy to ensure access to justice. It covered assistance with the cost of litigation and representation (legal aid), and of preliminary and non-contentious work (legal advice and assistance).

However, the demand-led nature of the scheme saw costs escalate while the proportion of the population eligible for help declined (creating the 'middle-income trap'—people not poor enough for legal aid but not wealthy enough to pay privately). The 1998 Modernising Justice White Paper detailed the main failings of the schemes:

(1) Civil legal aid was too heavily biased towards expensive court-based solutions.
(2) As lawyers were paid by work claimed, there was no incentive to deal with cases quickly and efficiently.
(3) While gross spending from 1993 to 1998 grew by 35 per cent (to approximately £800 million per year), the number of cases funded fell by 31 per cent—a third more money to help a third less people.
(4) Spending on criminal legal aid in the same period rose by 44 per cent while cases funded rose by only 10 per cent.
(5) The means test for criminal legal aid was a waste of time and money—it did not stop apparently wealthy defendants making successful claims, and 94 per cent of defendants in the Crown Court paid no contribution anyway.

How does the Community Legal Service work?

The Access to Justice Act 1999 abolished the legal aid scheme, establishing a Legal Services Commission to oversee a Community Legal Service (for civil matters) and a Criminal Defence Service (for criminal matters). The CLS funds access to civil legal services through contracts with lawyers and other providers (*e.g.* CAB). The CLS works with local authorities and others to establish Community Legal Service Partnerships to plan and co-ordinate the funding of local legal services. By March 2002 there were Partnerships covering over 95 per cent of the population. Access initiatives include the "Just Ask" website, and video-links between advice centres and remote communities. The merits test has been replaced by a new, more flexible funding assessment, encouraging alternative approaches (*e.g.* mediation) and alternative funding (*e.g.* conditional fees), though "litigation funding" is still available. The Act also improved and extended conditional fee arrangements, particularly by allowing the winning side to recover the success fee and legal insurance premiums from the losing side.

How does the Criminal Defence Service work?

The Criminal Defence Service uses a mixture of salaried public defenders and contracts with lawyers in private practice. This covers the full range of defence services, from advice at the police station to representation in court. The Duty Solicitor schemes at both police stations and magistrates' courts have been incorporated within the CDS. Complex and expensive cases, where the trial is expected to last at least 25 days, are covered by individual contracts with lawyers on a special panel who have demonstrated their competence to deal with such cases (*e.g.* complex fraud). The means test has been abolished, and judges have the power to order convicted defendants to pay some or all of their defence costs.

Have the reforms worked?

The use of subsidies to the private sector via legal aid offered no real, long-term solution to the unmet need for legal services. The AJA 1999 recognises that any successful strategy must employ a broader range of providers and funding. Overall, the changes mark a radical move towards the development of a more diverse, flexible and accessible range of services, funding and providers. However, it is not disputed that the unmet need persists. 2001 LSC research estimated that around one million victims of domestic violence, police mistreatment or medical negligence suffer in silence, because they are too scared to ask for help or believe they don't qualify for assistance. In 2003 the Law Society called for GP-style contracts for legal aid practices, recalling the never-implemented proposal for a national legal service by the 1945 Rushcliffe Committee on Legal Aid and Advice.

The AJA reforms, taken alongside the Woolf reforms of the civil justice, and proposals such as the introduction of further competition in the provision of conveyancing and probate services and the possible abolition of QCs, are part of the most radical overhaul of the legal system for at least half a century. The old legal aid system had become simply unsustainable, and the principles of diversity, flexibility and accessibility underlying the reforms are sensible. Whether they work remains to be seen.

15. CRIMINAL LAW: GENERAL PRINCIPLES

What are the basic elements of a crime?

Most crimes consist of an *actus reus* (physical element) and a *mens rea* (mental element). The actus reus can consist of conduct, circumstances, and consequences. **"Conduct" crimes** consist of conduct and circumstances—*e.g.* theft is the appropriation of property (conduct) belonging to another (circumstances). **"Result" crimes** consist of conduct and consequences—*e.g.* murder is an unlawful act (conduct) that causes the death of another human being (consequence).

What does "conduct" mean?

Generally, 'conduct' means a positive act—*i.e.* the defendant (D) must actually *do* something. There is no general criminal liability in English law (unlike, for example, French law) for omissions (a failure to act). For example, if a stranger sees a child drowning in a river and does nothing to rescue the child or raise the alarm, he does not commit a criminal offence. The fact that his conduct can be condemned on moral grounds does not make it illegal. However, this only applies to *pure* omissions. Where the omission is a failure to act where D is under a *duty to act*, then it is not *pure* and criminal liability may arise.

When does such a duty arise?

A duty to act can arise in a number of situations:

(1) It can be a **contractual** duty to act (*e.g. R v Pitwood* [1902]).
(2) It can be a **public** duty to act (*e.g. R v Dytham* [1979]).
(3) It can be a **parental** or **quasi-parental** duty to act (*e.g. R v Gibbins and Proctor* [1918]).
(4) It can arise from a **voluntary assumption of care** (*e.g. R v Stone and Dobinson* [1977]).
(5) It can arise from **"supervening fault"**, where D does nothing to rectify a dangerous situation created by their conduct (*e.g. R v Miller* [1982]; *DPP v Santana-Bermudez* [2003]).
(6) It can be a **statutory** duty to act (*e.g.* to report a road accident—Road Traffic Act 1988, s.170).

Should there be a general duty to act to prevent harm to others?

While there is a strong moral case for imposing a general duty that would, for example, apply in the 'drowning child' situation, there are a number of arguments *against* doing so:

(1) There are considerable difficulties in defining the nature and limits of such a duty. To what extent, for example, would someone be expected to put themselves at risk?

(2) It could require individuals to demonstrate an unreasonable level of heroism.

(3) It could expose the emergency services to unwarranted criminal liability.

(4) The proper role of the criminal law is to discourage bad behaviour rather than encourage good behaviour. It is one thing to punish people for being wicked, but something else to punish them for failing to be virtuous.

(5) There is a moral distinction between failures of commission (actively being bad) and failures of omission (failing to be good).

(6) On purely pragmatic grounds, the Criminal Justice System is busy enough trying to deal with those who are actively bad, without having to deal with those responsible for morally dubious omissions.

Therefore, the present approach of dealing with liability for omissions on a case-by-case basis seems the best way to proceed. This illustrates the benefits of an evolutionary, precedent-based approach, rather than trying to provide for all eventualities in a general Code.

What is the "requirement of causation" in "result" crimes?

Where the *actus reus* consists of both conduct and consequences, the prosecution must establish a **clear, unbroken causal link** between D's conduct and the unlawful consequence. This emphasises the fault-based nature of criminal liability—if D's conduct did not cause the unlawful consequence, then it is not his fault and he should not be liable for it. Establishing the causal link has *two* stages:

(1) D's conduct must be a "cause in fact" (or *sine qua non*) of the unlawful consequence—*i.e.* 'but for' D's conduct, the consequence would not have occurred. This applies even

where the conduct was intended, unsuccessfully, to cause the consequence (*R v White* [1910]).

(2) D's conduct must also be a "cause in law" of the unlawful consequence. This second requirement is necessary because some factual causes are too remote from the consequence to give rise to liability, and in some cases the actions of a third party (a *novus actus interveniens*) will break the link. While D's conduct need not be the sole or even the main cause (*R v Pagett* [1983]), it must make a significant contribution (*R v Cheshire* [1991]). The actions of a third party will only break the chain where their effect is so potent as to make D's contribution negligible (*R v Cheshire* [1991]).

It is also important to note that D must take his victim as he finds him—*i.e.* D cannot point to some unusual physical or mental characteristic of the victim in order to escape liability (*R v Blaue* [1975]). Also, D will be held to have caused (though not necessarily intended) all the reasonably foreseeable consequences of his conduct (*R v Pagett* [1983]; *R v Williams* [1992]).

Why are the rules on causation so strict?

It is true that it is very difficult for D to show that the actions of a third party are so significantly the cause of the unlawful consequence that this absolves D from any liability (contrast *R v Jordan* [1956] with *R v Smith* [1959] and *R v Cheshire* [1991]). This, together with rules such as "take your victim as you find", can sometimes seem to lead to harsh results. The courts seem to have developed such a strict set of rules largely for policy reasons: (a) that D should not be able to avoid the consequences of a chain of events in which their own unlawful conduct played a part, even if it not the main causative factor; (b) there is a risk that the public would perceive a less strict regime as allowing D to take advantage of legal technicalities to escape justice; (c) and that both these considerations are heightened by the fact that issues of causation tend to be most problematic in homicide cases.

Regarding the *mens rea*, what does "intention" mean?

Where the *mens rea* of a "result" crime requires proof of intention, this means an intention to bring about the unlawful consequence. There are *two* forms of intention:

(1) **Direct intent**—this is where it is D's *purpose* in acting to bring about the unlawful consequence.

(2) **Oblique intent**—this is where the unlawful consequence, although not D's purpose is: (a) *virtually certain* (barring some unforeseen intervention) to result from D's conduct; (b) D knows that it is virtually certain to result. (*R v Moloney* [1985]; *R v Hancock and Shankland* [1986]; *R v Nedrick* [1986]; *R v Woollin* [1998]).

Given its importance, it is surprising that the meaning of "intention" has caused the courts so many problems, particularly in relation to oblique intent. In *R v Moloney* [1985], Lord Bridge used the phrase "natural consequence". In *R v Hancock and Shankland* [1986], Lord Scarman said this was unsatisfactory because it lacked any reference to probability, but only added that the more probable the consequence, the more likely it was foreseen, and the more likely it was foreseen, the more likely it was intended. The trial judge in *R v Nedrick* [1986] attempted greater precision with the phrase "highly probable", but the Court of Appeal held this was not sufficient, and substituted "virtually certain". Finally, after the trial judge had used both "virtually certain" and "substantial risk" in *R v Woollin* [1998], the House of Lords confirmed that nothing less than "virtual certainty" will suffice.

It can be argued that the concept of oblique intent blurs the distinction between intention and recklessness. If a consequence is virtually certain, but not absolutely certain, then D can be seen as running a very high risk of causing it—*i.e.* as being highly reckless. However, given that the great majority of offences can be committed intentionally or recklessly, this debate is only important to offences that can only be committed intentionally, notably murder. In this respect, it may be argued that oblique intent serves a useful purpose in enabling those whose conduct shows such a high degree of disregard for human life to be convicted of murder rather than manslaughter.

Regarding the *mens rea*, what does "recklessness" mean?

Until recently there were *two* forms of recklessness:

(1) **Subjective recklessness**—this is where (a) D is subjectively aware there is a risk; (b) D nevertheless goes on to take that risk; and (c) the risk was objectively unjustified in the circumstances (*R v Cunningham* [1957]).

(2) **Objective recklessness**—this is where either (a) D is subjectively aware of the risk and nevertheless goes on to take it; *or* (b) D has given no thought to the possibility of the risk and the risk would have been obvious to a reasonable person; *and* (c) the risk was objectively unjustified in the circumstances (*R v Caldwell* [1981]). This test, after some uncertainty, was limited to criminal damage and some other modern statutory offences.

However, the concept of objective recklessness was heavily criticised:

(1) It was illogical and confusing to have two tests for the same concept.
(2) It blurred the distinction between recklessness and negligence. It can be argue that the fundamental difference between them is that recklessness requires conscious and deliberate risk-taking, whereas negligence only requires inadvertent or unthinking risk-taking.
(3) It extended negligence liability by the 'back door'.
(4) By excluding any reference to D's subjective characteristics, it could produce very harsh results (see, for example, *Elliott v C (a minor)* [1983]).
(5) The illogicality, complexity and potential unfairness of the test made it difficult for juries to understand and apply.

The House of Lords finally accepted these criticisms and, in *R v G and another* [2003], they used the 1966 Practice Statement to depart from their previous decision in *R v Caldwell* [1981] and revert to a single, subjective test.

How do the *actus reus* and *mens rea* relate to one another?

For liability to arise, D must have committed the actus reus while, at the same time, having the required *mens rea*—i.e. they must *coincide*. However, in order to prevent Ds taking advantage of a legal technicality, the courts have allowed some flexibility in meeting this requirement:

(1) Where the *actus reus* is of a *continuing* nature, then it is sufficient that D has the *mens rea* at some point during its commission (see, for example, *Fagan v MPC* [1968]).
(2) Where D has committed a series of related acts constituting a *single transaction*, it is sufficient that D has the *mens rea* at some point during that transaction (see, for exam-

ple, *Thabo Meli v R* [1954]; *R v Church* [1965]; *R v Le Brun* [1991]).

What if the intended victim and the actual victim of the crime are different?

In this situation, provided the intended offence and actual offence are of the same nature, the principle of "transferred malice" will apply. This transfers D's *mens rea* from his intended victim to his actual victim, again preventing D avoiding liability on a technicality (*R v Latimer* [1886]). Where D would have had a defence against his intended victim, this is also transferred to create a defence against the actual victim (*R v Gross* [1913]).

Is *mens rea* always required for a criminal offence?

As criminal liability is based upon the subjective fault of D, *mens rea* would seem essential. However, the law does recognise some **offences of strict liability**, where there is no requirement of *mens rea* in relation to one or more aspects of the *actus reus* (see, for example, *R v Marriott* [1971]). Almost all of these offences are created by statute and, because they are contrary to general principle, the courts have been very reluctant to recognise them (see *Sweet v Parsley* [1970]; *B (a minor) v DPP* [2000]; *R v K* [2001]).

How can we recognise strict liability offences?

In *Gammon v A-G of Hong Kong* [1984], Lord Scarman gave clear guidance on this issue:

> ➤ There is a presumption of *mens rea* when interpreting criminal statutes.
> ➤ This is particularly strong where the offence is "truly criminal".
> ➤ It can only be displaced where Parliament's intention to impose strict liability is clear.
> ➤ This is only possible where the statute deals with an issue of social concern.
> ➤ Even then, it is only possible where strict liability would encourage greater care.

Therefore, it seems that strict liability offences fall into *two* categories:

(1) **Regulatory offences** (*e.g.* parking offences) that are not 'truly criminal'.
(2) **Public interest offences** (*e.g.* dangerous drugs, environmental pollution—*Alphacell v Woodward* [1972]).

Can strict liability be justified in the criminal law?

The arguments *against* strict liability are:

(1) It is contrary to general principle.
(2) It serves no purpose to criminalise those who have taken reasonable care to comply with the law.
(3) It can result in unfair stigmatisation.

The arguments *for* its limited use are:

(1) There are circumstances (*e.g.* public health issues or environmental protection) where the public interest in prohibition outweighs the individual interest protected by the requirement of *mens rea*.
(2) It can encourage positive steps to ensure compliance with the law, rather than merely negative steps to avoid non-compliance.
(3) It avoids the complications that would otherwise arise in establishing corporate criminal liability.
(4) While fault is not relevant to liability, it remains relevant to sentencing.
(5) Strict liability is not absolute liability, and D may still be able to raise a defence.
(6) In many cases, the statute will provide for a "due diligence" defence, effectively making the offence one of negligence liability rather than strict liability.

16. CRIMINAL LAW: GENERAL DEFENCES

When is automatism a defence?

Here, the defendant (D) argues that they had no conscious, voluntary control over their actions—*i.e.* that they were in an automotive state. The cause of the automotive state must be *external* (*e.g.* a blow to the head, the effects of medication) rather than internal (*e.g.* any illness affecting mental function or a mental disorder) (contrast *R v Quick* [1973] with *R v Hennessy* [1989]). Contrary to its use in the past as a "classic" example, sleepwalking is *not* such an external factor (*R v Burgess* [1991]). Also, the defence is *not* available where the automotive state is self-induced through the voluntary consumption of dangerous drugs (*R v Lipman* [1969]).

When is insanity a defence?

Insanity here is a legal, not medical concept. Under the M'Naghten Rules [1843], *three* requirements must be met:

(1) D must have been suffering from a **"defect of reason"**—*i.e.* total deprivation of the power to reason (*R v Clarke* [1972]).

(2) This must have been caused by a **"disease of the mind"**—*i.e.* any illness, disease or other internal factor that impairs mental function. This can include not only mental disorders but also diseases such as arteriosclerosis (*R v Kemp* [1957]), epilepsy (*R v Sullivan* [1983]), diabetes (*R v Hennessy* [1989]), and somnambulism (*R v Burgess* [1991]).

(3) With the result that *either* D did not know the physical nature of what he was doing (*i.e.* was in an automotive state or suffering from insane delusions) *or*, if he did know, he did not know that it was wrong (*i.e.* contrary to law—*R v Windle* [1952]—*e.g.* D was suffering from insane delusions which, if true, would have made their conduct lawful).

If successful, this defence results not in an acquittal but in the special verdict of "not guilty by reason of insanity", giving the court wide discretion in disposal from an absolute discharge to detention in hospital (Criminal Procedure (Insanity and Unfitness to Plead) Act 1991).

How satisfactory are these 'mental state' defences?

The present law is subject to a number of criticisms:

    [X] It is based on outmoded notions of mental conditions.

☓ While the policy is sensible—attempting to distinguish between Ds who though not criminally at fault nevertheless represent a continuing danger to themselves or the public, from those who do not—the means adopted (the internal/external distinction) is a rather crude mechanism.

☓ This can lead to some absurd and/or undesirable classifications—*e.g.* regarding diabetes and epilepsy.

A better approach would be to have a single special verdict of "not guilty by reason of automatism" where D is not mentally responsible (for whatever reason) for the conduct, enabling the court to deal with D in the most appropriate way following medical/social reports. Any such development would have to be legislative rather than judicial (*R v Sullivan* [1983]).

When is mistake a defence?

A mistake of fact (NOT law) may be a defence where its effect is such that D did not form the required mens rea. In *all* cases the mistake must be an *honest* one, and in *some* instances it must also be *reasonable—R v Williams* [1987]:

(1) Where intention or subjective recklessness is required, the mistake need only be honest, it need not also be reasonable (though the more unreasonable, the less likely it was honestly made).

(2) Where negligence is required, the mistake must be both honest and reasonable.

(3) Where the offence is one of strict liability, mistake is no defence.

Also, mistake is no defence where it results from voluntary intoxication (*R v O'Grady* [1987]).

When is intoxication a defence?

Intoxication has proved a problematic defence. As a matter of *principle*, it should be a defence where D does not form the *mens rea*. However, as a matter of *policy* it is wrong that intoxicated offenders should be able to avoid responsibility for the actions, particularly as so many offences are committed 'in drink'. Therefore, the law represents an uneasy compromise between these two competing imperatives:

(1) **Involuntary intoxication** (where D has been forced to consume the intoxicant or has consumed it in ignorance of its intoxicating properties) *is* a defence to any crime where D, taking his intoxication into account, did not form the required *mens rea* (*R v Sheehan* [1975]; *R v Pordage* [1975]). It is *not* a defence where despite the intoxication D did form the *mens rea*, even if the effect of the intoxication was to reduce sober inhibitions (*R v Kingston* [1994]). Intoxication is *not* involuntary where D knows the substance to be intoxicating but is mistaken as to its strength (*R v Allen* [1988]).

(2) **Voluntary intoxication** (where D voluntary consumes a known intoxicant) *is* a defence to crimes of *specific* intent (but *not* to crimes of *basic* intent) where D, taking his intoxication into account, did not form the required *mens rea* (*DPP v Majewski* [1976]; *R v Lipman* [1969]). Specific intent crimes include crimes of ulterior intent (where the *mens rea* extend beyond the *actus reus*—e.g. theft), attempts, and murder. All other crimes, including manslaughter, are basic intent crimes.

(3) **Dutch courage**—voluntary intoxication is *not* a defence where D has consumed the intoxicant in order to overcome sober inhibitions (*Attorney-General for Northern Ireland v Gallagher* [1963]).

(4) ***Bona fide* medical use**—voluntary intoxication may be a defence to *any* crime where the intoxicant (whether prescribed or not) was consumed for *bona fide* medical purposes, provided (a) its effect is normally sedative or stabilising; (b) D was not subjectively reckless as to a risk it might induce aggressive, unpredictable or uncontrollable conduct (*R v Bailey* [1983]; *R v Hardie* [1984]).

While the above may seem inconsistent, illogical, and complex, it is a serious attempt by the courts to temper principle with pragmatism. Arguably the only alternative would be the minority recommendation of the Criminal Law Revision Committee's 14th report for a special verdict or "guilty while intoxicated", shifting the relevance of intoxication from liability to sentencing.

When is duress by threats a defence?

In order to establish this defence, D must show (*R v Graham* [1982]; *R v Howe* [1986]):

(1) They were/may have been forced to act as they did because, as a result of what they reasonably believed the threatener to have said or done, they had good cause to fear that if they did not the threatener would kill them or cause them serious injury; AND

(2) A sober person of reasonable firmness, in the circumstances as D reasonably believed them to be and sharing such of D's characteristics as would affect the gravity of the threat to them, would/may have responded in the same way.

The defence is also available where the threat is aimed at someone D is under a duty to protect (*R v Shayler* [2001]). Also, while the threat must be an operative factor on D's mind, it need not be the sole factor (*R v Valderrama-Vega* [1985]). However, the defence is *not* available where:

(1) D had a reasonable opportunity to avoid the threatened consequences. However, while the threat must be imminent (*i.e.* operative on D's mind at the time of committing the offence), it need not be capable of immediate execution (*R v Hudson & Taylor* [1971]; *R v Abdul-Hussain & others* [1999]). It is sufficient that D reasonably believed there was a threat—it is not necessary to show that the threat in fact existed (*R v Safi & others* [2003]).

(2) The threat comes from an organisation joined voluntarily by D in the knowledge that threats of death/serious injury might be used to compel them to commit offences of the type charged (*R v Sharp* [1987]; *R v Shepherd* [1988]; *R v Z* [2003]).

(3) There is an insufficient connection (nexus) between the threat and the offence (*R v Cole* [1994]).

(4) The offence charged is murder (*R v Howe* [1987]) or attempted murder (*R v Gotts* [1992]).

When is duress of circumstances a defence?

In order to establish this defence, D must show (*R v Willer* [1986]; *R v Conway* [1988]; *R v Martin* [1989]; *R v Pommell* [1995]):

(1) They were/may have been forced to act as they did because, as a result of what they reasonably believed the circumstances to be, they had good cause to fear that if

they did not they would be killed or suffer serious injury; AND

(2) A sober person of reasonable firmness, in the circumstances as D reasonably believed them to be and sharing such of D's characteristics as would affect the gravity of the threat to them, would/may have responded in the same way.

The causative circumstances must be external to D (*R v Rodger & Rose* [1998]), and the defence is subject to the same limitations as duress by threats (see above).

When is necessity a defence?

While it was thought that English law did not recognise any general defence of necessity (*R v Dudley & Stephens* [1884]; *London Borough of Southwark v Williams* [1971]), two recent decisions have cast some doubt on this. Following the decision in *Re A (children) (conjoined twins: surgical separation)* [2000], the Court of Appeal in *R v Shayler* [2001] stated that D would have a defence where:

(1) The act was necessary to avoid an imminent threat of death or serious injury to D or someone for whom they reasonably regard themselves as responsible.
(2) The act done was no more than reasonably necessary to avoid the harm feared.
(3) The harm caused was not disproportionate to the harm feared.

This seems to be very similar in all material respects to the two forms of the duress defence. What is not clear is whether this necessity defence would be available to murder or attempted murder. While *Re A* indicates that it might be, the more likely position, following *Dudley & Stephens*, is that it is not.

How satisfactory are these "necessity" defences?

The issues to be considered are:

(1) The courts' reluctance to recognise anything other than very limited forms of necessity defence due to a fear that (as Lord Denning stated in *Williams*) this "would open a

way through which all kinds of disorder and lawlessness would pass. . . The plea would be an excuse for all sorts of wrongdoing".

(2) The basis of the defences as a "concession to human frailty", recognising that in extreme circumstances, people may feel compelled to commit an offence as the lesser of two evils.

(3) Whether the various limitations outlined above achieve a satisfactory balance between these two positions.

(4) In particular, whether the murder/attempted murder exception can be justified. It may be that murder is a unique offence meriting exceptional treatment. On the other hand, this may demand an unreasonable level of heroism. It is also inconsistent that the defences are available to a charge of GBH with intent, the mens rea of which is also sufficient for murder. This would not be an issue if the mandatory life sentence for murder was abolished. Alternatively, killing under duress/necessity could become a category of voluntary manslaughter.

(5) Whether it would be better to abolish the defences, leaving any issues of duress or necessity to prosecutorial discretion and/or sentencing mitigation.

When is self-defence a defence?

A person may use force in self-defence to repel a violent, unlawful or indecent assault. *Both* the decision to use force *and* the degree of force used must be reasonable in the circumstances as D honestly (even if mistakenly) believed them to be (*R v Williams* [1987]; *R v Owino* [1995]), taking into account the time available to consider what to do (the "heat of the moment" factor) (*Palmer v R* [1971]). Whether the degree of force used is proportionate to that faced, and whether D sought to retreat, are simply factors to be considered in deciding whether D's conduct was reasonable in the circumstances (*R v Bird* [1985]). Similar principles govern acting in defence of another and acting in defence of property, and there is considerable overlap with the statutory defence of acting in the prevention of crime under the Criminal Law Act 1967, *s.3*.

The main issue here is the 'all or nothing' nature of the defence. In particular, where D's decision to use force is reasonable but they then use an unreasonable or excessive degree of force, thus being deprived of the defence. While this is partly addressed by the 'heat of the moment' factor, and with most offences can also be accommodated through sentencing discretion, the mandatory life sentence for murder is once again problematic (see *R v Clegg* [1995] and *R v Martin* [2001]). It is for this reason that the *2003 Law Commission consultation paper on partial defences to murder* examines whether excessive and fatal force in reasonable self-defence should be added to the categories of voluntary manslaughter.

When is the consent of the victim a defence?

Generally, consent of the victim is no defence. However, it may be a defence to common assault where the activity involved is not contrary to the public interest (*R v Donovan* [1934]; *Attorney-General's Reference (No.6 of 1980)* [1981]). It may also be a defence to the reckless causing of more serious harm where the victim consented to the risk of such injury (*R v Dica* [2004]), but not to the intentional causing of such harm (*R v Brown* [1993]; *R v Wilson* [1996]; *R v Emmett* [1999]; *R v Dica* [2004]). It may also be a defence to a serious assault in *two* further situations:

(1) Surgical treatment.
(2) Sports and games—players are held to consent to contact both integral and incidental to the sport (including some foul play, but not deliberate foul play nor contact entirely unrelated to the sport) (*R v Billinghurst* [1978]). This extends beyond organised sport to include rough and undisciplined play, provided there was no intention to cause harm (*R v Jones* [1986]).

The victim's consent must be genuine. This is clearly not so when procured by duress or by a deception as to D's identity. However, any other deception will not vitiate the victim's consent where they had nevertheless consented to *both* the nature *and* quality of the act (although this involves making some very fine, and arguably unsustainable distinctions—see *R v Richardson* [1999]; *R v Tabassum* [2000]; *R v Dica* [2004]). Also, consent obtained by fraud is no defence where fraud is an element of the offence itself (*R v Cort* [2003]).

There are *three* main issues regarding consent:

(1) The law is complex to understand and difficult to apply consistently.

(2) Consensual sexual activity in private—while some would argue that law has "no place in the bedroom", others would support legal intervention on moral or public health grounds (see *R v Brown* [1993]; *R v Dica* [2004]).

(3) Euthanasia—while the courts have faced some difficult cases (*e.g. R v Cox* [1992]; *Airedale NHS Trust v Bland* [1993]; *R v DPP, ex parte Diane Pretty* [2001]), active euthanasia or "mercy killing" remains murder at common law. Any alteration to this is properly the province of Parliament, not the courts.

17. CRIMINAL LAW: MURDER AND MANSLAUGHTER

What is the *actus reus* of murder?

The actus reus of murder is an **unlawful act**—normally, but not necessarily, a direct assault by the defendant (D) on the victim (V)—that causes the death of another human being. It used to be a requirement (to resolve issues of causation) that the death must occur within a year and a day. However, this requirement was abolished by the Law Reform (Year and a Day Rule) Act 1996. Now, the Attorney-General's consent is required for a murder prosecution where the death occurs more than three years later or where D has already been convicted of an offence (*e.g.* GBH) committed in circumstances connected with the death.

What is the *mens rea* of murder?

The *mens rea* of murder is traditionally referred to as **malice aforethought**, and there are *two* forms (*R v Moloney* [1985]):

(1) An intention to kill (*express malice*).

(2) An intention to cause really serious injury (*implied malice*). There is no need to show D also foresaw a risk of death—it is sufficient that D intended to cause really serious injury and that death, in fact, resulted (*R v Vickers* [1957]).

There are *two* main issues relating to murder:

(1) That the *mens rea* is too broad and should be limited to express malice. Regarding implied malice, whether V only suffers serious injury or dies is often a matter of chance, unrelated to D's intentions. Therefore, the more appropriate offence would be manslaughter, particularly where implied malice is coupled with oblique intent. Against this, it can be argued that someone who acts with an obvious disregard for human life should be convicted of murder.

(2) That the mandatory life sentence for murder should be replaced by a discretionary life sentence, allowing the judge to impose a sentence appropriate to the offender (contrast, for example, the culpability of the contract killer or terrorist with that of the "mercy killer"). The mandatory sentence is largely a matter of historical accident, a consequence of building the parliamentary coalition necessary to abolish the death penalty. This would also have the advantage of removing the need for the different categories of voluntary manslaughter, leaving factors such as provocation to be treated as mitigation.

What is voluntary manslaughter?

Voluntary manslaughter is killing with malice aforethought (*i.e.* murder) where D can raise one of the *three* special and partial defences under the Homicide Act 1957:

(1) **Diminished responsibility** (Homicide Act 1957, s.2)—D must show that:
  ➢ He was suffering from an **"abnormality of mind"** (whether due to internal or external factors)—this is a state of mind so different from that of ordinary people that a reasonable person would regard it as abnormal, including not only impairments of reason and perception but also of the ability to exercise will-power (*R v Byrne* [1960]).
  ➢ That this **substantially impaired his mental responsibility** for the killing—a substantial impairment is one that is more than trivial but need not be total (*R v Lloyd* [1967]).

In October 2003 the Law Commission published a consultation paper on partial defences to murder that identifies the main issues relating to diminished responsibility:

☒ The vagueness and uncertainty surrounding the defence has enabled it to become a convenient way of ensuring those who are not thought to deserve the mandatory life sentence (*e.g.* those who commit "mercy killings") are found guilty of manslaughter rather than murder.

☒ It is an anomaly, as it is not a defence (either full or partial) to any other offence.

☒ It is an ill-defined compromise, introduced in the era of the death penalty to ensure someone with an obvious lack of mental capacity but who did not meet the strict legal test for insanity was not convicted of murder. If the mandatory life sentence were abolished, then the various circumstances that can give rise to the defence could simply be regarded as mitigation.

☒ It can be complex and confusing for juries. For example, while diminished responsibility can result from alcoholism, it cannot arise from temporary intoxication (*R v Tandy* [1988]). Therefore, where D pleads diminished responsibility on the basis of, for example, severe depression, but was also intoxicated at the time of the killing, then the jury is faced with the impossible task of considering what D would or may have done in the circumstances had they not been intoxicated (*R v Gittens* [1984]; *R v Dietschmann* [2003]).

☑ Even if the mandatory life sentence were abolished, the partial defence would still be needed for "fair labelling" of D. Against this, it could be argued that someone who kills with malice aforethought, even if their responsibility is diminished in some way, should be labelled a murderer.

☑ The defence has been generally satisfactory in practice. The fact that it is sometimes used sympathetically is not a good reason to abolish it. Against this, it could be argued that mitigation of sentence is the correct place for the exercise of sympathy.

(2) **Provocation** (Homicide Act 1957, s.3)—D must satisfy *two* elements:

➢ The **subjective** element—that as a result of things said, done or both together, he was provoked to lose his self-control. The loss of self-control must be "sudden and temporary" (*R v Duffy* [1949]), but need not be immediate ("slow-burn" provocation—*R v Ahluwalia* [1992]). Also, any prior history of provocation is a relevant consideration ("last straw" provocation—*R v Thornton* [1922]).

➤ The **objective** element—that a reasonable man in the same circumstances (including any prior history) would or may have been provoked to lose his self-control (the "control" element) and would or may have responded in the same way (the "response" element). The "reasonable man" is someone of the same age and sex as D, and sharing such other of D's characteristics as would affect the gravity of the provocation to him (*DPP v Camplin* [1978]). These characteristics are relevant to both the control and response elements (*R v Smith* [2000]). Whether a characteristic is relevant (apart from unusual volatility or intoxication, which cannot be relied on) is "all a matter for the jury" (*R v Weller* [2003]; *R v Rowland* [2003]). The question for the jury is whether or not D's loss of self control was sufficiently excusable to reduce murder to manslaughter (*JSB model direction*, approved in *Rowland*).

Provocation may still be a defence where the provocation comes from a third party rather than the victim (*R v Davies* [1975]), where it is aimed at a third party rather than D (*R v Pearson* [1992]), and even where it is self-induced by D's own conduct (*R v Johnson* [1989]).

The 2003 Law Commission paper also identified the main problems with the provocation defence:

- ☒ It is inherently contradictory to suggest that killing may be a "reasonable" response to provocation, however extreme.
- ☒ The effect of the decisions in *Smith*, *Weller* and *Rowland* is to remove any pretence of an objective element, leaving the matter entirely to the moral judgement of the jury, with the attendant risk of inconsistency and injustice.
- ☒ It makes a concession towards one particular (and not very creditable) emotion, anger, while no similar concession is made towards other (and perhaps more

creditable) emotions, such as fear, despair, or compassion.

[X] This in turn makes the defence gender-biased as men are more likely than women to kill as a result of sudden rage, often fuelled by jealousy, and may serve to perpetuate male violence towards women (there are approximately 100 domestic killings each year, 95 per cent of which are committed by men).

[X] It blames the victim for the murder, who obviously has no opportunity to counter D's version of events. By showing (arguably misplaced) compassion towards D, the law fails to show due respect for the life of V.

Therefore, the better solution may be, as with diminished responsibility, to couple abolition of the defence and of the mandatory life sentence, leaving any provocation as a matter of mitigation (as it is for all other offences).

(3) **Suicide pacts** (Homicide Act 1957, s.4)—it is manslaughter where D kills V as part of a suicide pact between them. A suicide pact is an agreement between two or more persons having as its object the death of all of them. The defence is only available where D's acts were done while he had a settled intention of dying in pursuance of the pact.

What is involuntary manslaughter?

Involuntary manslaughter is killing without malice aforethought, and takes *two* forms (*R v Adomako* [1994]):

(1) **Constructive (unlawful act) manslaughter**—the *actus reus* is the commission of an unlawful and dangerous act that causes the death of another. The act must be *both* unlawful *and* dangerous (*R v Slingsby* [1995]), and dangerous in the sense that it exposes another to the risk of some harm, albeit not serious harm (*R v Church* [1965]). The *mens rea* is that required for the unlawful act. It is not necessary to show D knew the act was unlawful or dangerous—it is sufficient that this would have been obvious to a reasonable man (*DPP v Newbury and Jones* [1976]).

(2) **Gross negligence manslaughter**—the *actus reus* is a breach of duty owed by D towards V that causes the death of V. The existence of the duty is a question of law

for the judge (*R v Singh* [1999]). The mens rea is gross negligence—*i.e.* that the breach of duty is so bad, having regard to the risk of death involved, as to amount in the jury's opinion to a criminal act or omission (*R v Adomako* [1994]). In *R v Lidar* [1999] it was stated that there had to be a high probability of serious injury and that D took that risk either advertantly (*i.e.* recklessly) or inadvertently (*i.e.* negligently).

In 2000, the Government published a consultation paper on involuntary manslaughter (based on a 1996 Law Commission report) that identified the criticisms of the present law and *three* replacement offences:

- ☒ The gross negligence test is circular, in that it invites juries to convict if they think D's conduct was criminal.
- ☒ The scope of constructive manslaughter is too broad, ranging from conduct that is little more than an accident to that which is little short of murder. This creates problems for judges in determining sentence and for the public in understanding why a particular sentence has been passed.

(1) **Reckless killing**—where (a) D's conduct causes the death of another; (b) D is aware his conduct creates a risk of death or serious injury; and (c) it is unreasonable in the circumstances to take that risk.

(2) **Killing by gross carelessness**—where (a) D's conduct causes the death of another; (b) a risk of death or serious injury would have been obvious to a reasonable person; (c) D was capable of appreciating that risk but did not in fact do so; and *either* (d) D's conduct falls far below that which could reasonably be expected *or* (e) he intends to cause some injury, or is aware of and unreasonably takes a risk of doing so, and the injury is unlawful.

(3) **Death resulting from the intentional or reckless causing of minor injury**—where (a) D's conduct causes the death of another; (b) D intends or is reckless as to causing some injury (although death or serious injury was *not* foreseeable); and (c) D's conduct is unlawful.

18. CRIMINAL LAW: NON-FATAL ASSAULTS

What is "common assault"?

Common assault is an offence contrary to the Criminal Justice Act 1988, s.39, and embraces the old common law offences of assault and battery. The *actus reus* is:

(1) Placing another in fear of immediate personal violence (assault), either by words, deeds, conduct, menacing silence (*R v Ireland & Burstow* [1997]), or omission (*DPP v Santana-Bermudez* [2003]); OR

(2) The application of force on another (battery). Any degree of non-consensual contact is sufficient (though we are held to impliedly consent to contact generally acceptable in the ordinary conduct of daily life).

The *mens rea* is intention or subjective recklessness as to the assault or battery (*R v Venna* [1976]).

What is "ABH"?

Assault occasioning "Actual Bodily Harm" is an offence contrary to the Offences Against the Person Act 1861, s.47. The *actus reus* is an assault that causes actual bodily harm (harm that is more than trivial but not really serious—*DPP v Smith* [1961]). "Bodily" harm includes both physical and mental injury (but not mere emotions such as fear, distress, or panic—*R v Chan-Fook* [1994]). Following *R v Dica* [2004], ABH also includes the transmission of disease. The *mens rea* is the same as for common assault—there is no need to show the defendant (D) intended or foresaw that ABH might be caused (*R v Savage & Parmenter* [1991]).

What is "GBH"?

Unlawful and malicious wounding or inflicting "Grievous Bodily Harm" is an offence contrary to the OAPA, s.20. The *actus reus* is *either* wounding (breaking the inner and outer skin—*Moriarty v Brookes* [1834]) *or* causing really serious injury (*DPP v Smith* [1961]). "Injury" includes both physical and mental injury (*R v Ireland & Burstow* [1997]) and the transmission of disease (*R v Dica* [2004]). The *mens rea* is intention or subjective recklessness as to causing some harm, albeit not serious harm—there is no need to show that D intended or foresaw that serious harm might be caused (*R v Savage & Parmenter* [1991]).

What is "GBH with intent"?

Unlawful and malicious wounding or causing Grievous Bodily Harm with intent to do so or to resist arrest is an offence contrary to the OAPA, s.18. The *actus reus* is the same as that for s.18. The *mens rea* is *either* an intention to wound or cause GBH *or* intention to resist arrest and either intention or subjective recklessness as to causing some harm albeit not serious harm.

How satisfactory is the present law on non-fatal assaults?

The main criticisms of the OAPA are:

- ☒ It was a consolidation of existing, older law. As such, the language is archaic and inconsistent (*e.g.* "occasioning", "inflicting", etc).
- ☒ There is a confusing lack of symmetry between the *actus reus* and *mens rea* of some offences (*e.g.* ss.20 and 47).
- ☒ The scope of "bodily harm" continues to be problematic (*e.g.* whether it does/should cover transmission of disease).
- ☒ The inclusion of "wounding" confuses the manner of harm with the degree of harm caused (which ought to be the sole determinant).
- ☒ s.18 is confused by the inclusion of additional protection for the police within the general offence.

All this causes problems of interpretation and application for the police, prosecutors, courts, and juries, leading to expensive and unnecessary appeals and a risk of injustice for both victims and defendants. Following a 1993 Law Commission Report, the Home Office published a consultation paper and draft Bill in 1998. This proposed four new principal offences:

(1) Intentionally causing serious injury (including by omission) (Clause 1). "Injury" included both physical and mental injury, and for the purposes of Clause 1 *only*, the transmission of disease (Clause 15).

(2) Recklessly causing serious injury (requiring foresight of serious injury, thus restoring symmetry to the *actus reus* and *mens rea*) (Clause 2). Recklessness is defined subjectively (Clause 14).

(3) Intentionally or recklessly causing injury (requiring intention or foresight of some injury, thus restoring symmetry to the *actus reus* and *mens rea*) (Clause 3).

(4) Assault (the intentional or reckless application of force or intentionally or recklessly causing another to fear imminent force) (Clause 4).

The advantages of these changes would be:

☑ They modernise and simplify the language used.
☑ They restore symmetry to the *actus reus* and *mens rea* of the various offences.
☑ The scope of "injury" is clearly defined, avoiding criminalising the reckless transmission of minor ailments.
☑ The degree of harm caused is the sole determinant.
☑ Additional protection for the police is provided in separate offences (Clauses 5–7).

However, because these proposals have not been enacted, the courts have been left to deal with the problems of the 1861 Act (*e.g.* assaults by omission—*DPP v Sanata-Bermudez* [2003]), sometimes arriving at consequences that contradict the government's proposals (*e.g.* the effect of *R v Dica* [2004] may be to criminalise the reckless transmission of minor ailments under s.47). Therefore, the law is in even more "urgent need of reform" than the Home Office thought in 1998.

---

19. CRIMINAL LAW: PROPERTY OFFENCES

What is 'theft'?

Under the Theft Act 1968, s.1, the *actus reus* of theft is the appropriation of property belonging to another, and the *mens rea* is dishonesty and an intention to permanently deprive the other of the property. Further guidance on each of these elements is contained in ss.2–6.

What does "appropriation" mean?

An appropriation is any assumption of any of the rights of the owner (TA, s.3, *R v Morris* [1983]) (and includes where someone comes by the property without stealing it, any later assumption by keeping or dealing with it as owner). It does not matter whether this was done with or without the consent of the owner (*Lawrence v MPC* [1971]), whether the consent was obtained by a deception (*R v Gomez* [1993]), or even that the owner has made a valid gift of the property (*R v Hinks* [2000]). This very broad interpretation of "appropriation" has been the subject of debate and disagreement in the House of Lords:

(1) The **majority** position—Viscount Dilhorne (speaking for a unanimous court in *Lawrence*) held that the issue of permission or consent was irrelevant. Lord Keith (for the majority in *Gomez*) confirmed this view, adding that the fact that the same conduct would also ground a charge of obtaining property by deception (TA, s.15) was equally irrelevant. Lord Steyn (for the majority in *Hinks*) stated that this approach was necessary as any other interpretation would "place beyond the reach of the criminal law dishonest persons who should be found guilty of theft".

(2) The **minority position**—Lord Roskill (speaking for a unanimous court in *Morris*) argued that appropriation involved an element of adverse interference with or usurpation of the owner's rights. Lord Lowry (in *Gomez*) took a similar view, drawing on the Criminal Law Revision Committee report that preceded the Act, that an appropriation was a one-sided or unilateral act, pointing out that the appropriate charge where consent was obtained by fraud was under s.15, not s.1. Lord Hobhouse (in *Hinks*) stated that to treat conduct as criminal simply because the court or jury regard it as immoral is to reduce theft to a vague and subjective offence (a view supported by the 2002 Law Commission Report on Fraud), pointing out that while theft is a crime of dishonesty, dishonesty is not the only element of the offence. Strangely, the Court of Appeal in *R v Briggs* [2003] seems to have preferred this minority position (although the decision may simply be per incuriam).

What does "property" mean?

Under TA, s.4, "property" includes money and all other real or personal property (including intangible property, such as a debt). Land (and things severed from land), however, generally cannot be stolen unless:

(1) The defendant (D) was dealing with the land as trustee or equivalent.
(2) D, not being in possession of the land, appropriates something from the land by severing it or after it has been severed.
(3) D, being a tenant, appropriates any structure let with the land.
(4) D appropriates wild flowers, fruit, plants or mushrooms growing on the land for reward, sale or other commercial purpose.

What does "belonging to another" mean?

Under TA, s.5, property 'belongs' to anyone who has possession or control of it, or has any proprietary right or interest in it (so that D can, in appropriate circumstances, steal his own property—*R v Turner* [1971]). Property is also regarded as belonging to another where:

(1) D is a trustee.
(2) D receives the property under an obligation to keep and deal with it in a particular way (*e.g. Davidge v Bunnett* [1984]).
(3) D receives the property through another's mistake and is under an obligation to return it (*e.g. Attorney-General's Reference (No.1 of 1983)* [1984]).

What does "dishonesty" mean?

The TA does not provide any general definition of dishonesty. However, s.2 provides that someone is *not* dishonest where:

(1) They believe they have a legal right to deprive the other of it.
(2) They believe the other would consent if he knew of the appropriation and its circumstances.
(3) They believe the person to whom the property belongs cannot be identified by taking reasonable steps.

In all other circumstances, a person is dishonest where (*R v Ghosh* [1983]):

(1) Their conduct would be regarded as dishonest by the ordinary standards of reasonable and honest people (the objective element); AND
(2) They knew that their conduct was so regarded (even if they did not regard it as dishonest by their own standards) (the subjective element).

How satisfactory is the "Ghosh" approach?

The problem here is that a purely objective test would regard as dishonest some people who clearly are not (see Lord Lane's example of the foreign tourist on the bus in *Ghosh*), while a purely objective test would open the way for so-called "Robin Hood" defences (see Lord Lane's example of the ardent anti-vivisectionists in *Ghosh*). Some have criticised the "Ghosh" compromise:

- ☒ It requires the jury to engage in a moral enquiry.
- ☒ This creates a risk of inconsistency and injustice.

However, the 2002 Law Commission Report on Fraud observes that:

- ☑ It provides a structured, two-stage approach to the question.
- ☑ It prevents 'Robin Hood' defences.
- ☑ It requires fact-finders (magistrates and juries) to measure D's conduct according to what they perceive as the moral norms of society at large, *not* the fact-finders own moral views, thus reducing the scope for inconsistency.
- ☑ The Commission is unaware of any more precise definition that could be used.
- ☑ The "Ghosh" approach has proved to be unproblematic in practice. Therefore, in the Commission's view, any risk of inconsistency is a theoretical one.

What does "intention to permanently deprive" mean?

Under TA, s.6, it is immaterial whether the appropriation is made with a view to gain or for D's own benefit—what matters is that D intends the other person to be permanently deprived of the property. In most cases, this is unproblematic. However, there are three situations which need further clarification under s.6:

(1) **Abandoning the property**—D is regarded as having an intention to permanently deprive, notwithstanding that they do not mean the other to permanently lose the thing itself, if they treat the property as their own to dispose of regardless of the other's rights.

(2) **Borrowing or lending the property** will only amount to an intention to permanently deprive where it is for a period and in circumstances that amount to an outright taking or disposal (*i.e.* that although the thing itself is returned, it is in such a changed state that all its goodness or virtue has gone—*R v Lloyd* [1985]).

(3) **Pawning the property**—D is regarded as treating the property as their own to dispose of regardless of the other's rights where they part with the property under a condition as to its return that they may not be able to perform.

What is "robbery"?

Under TA, s.8, the *actus reus* of robbery is that of theft plus the use or threat of immediate force. The force/threat of force must take place immediately before or at the time of the theft (see *R v Hale* [1979]; *R v Lockley* [1995]) and must be done in order to steal. The *mens rea* is that for theft plus an intention to use force/threat of force in order to steal.

What is "burglary"?

Under TA, s.9, there are *two* forms of burglary:

	s.9(1)(a)	s.9(1)(b)
Actus reus	• Entering (see *R v Collins* [1972]; *R v Brown* [1985]; *R v Ryan* [1996]) • A building or part of a building (including any inhabited vehicle or vessel) (see *R v Walkington* [1979]) • As a trespasser (including exceeding the scope of any permission to enter — see *R v Jones & Smith* [1976]).	• As for s.9(1)(a), *and*: • The *actus reus* of theft/attempted theft; *or* • The *actus reus* of GBH/attempted GBH.

Mens rea	• Intention or subjective recklessness as to the trespass. • An intention to steal, inflict GBH, rape, or commit criminal damage.	• Intention or subjective recklessness as to the trespass. • The *mens rea* of theft/attempted theft; OR • Where GBH is inflicted, the *mens rea* of either a s.20 or s.18 GBH; OR • Where GBH is attempted, the *mens rea* of a s.18 GBH.

What is "obtaining property by deception"?

Under TA, s.15, the *actus reus* of obtaining property by deception is obtaining (*i.e.* obtaining ownership, possession or control) of property (including land) belonging to another (see above) by deception (a false representation—express or implied (*R v Laverty* [1970]; *MPC v Charles* [1977]; *R v Lambie* [1981]) by words or conduct—as to fact, law, or present intention that induces the other person to allow or enable the obtaining). The *mens rea* is intention or subjective recklessness as to the deception (*Large v Mainprize* [1989]; *R v Goldman* [1997]), "Ghosh" dishonesty, and an intention to permanently deprive the other of the property (see above).

What is "obtaining services by deception"?

Under the Theft Act 1978, s.1, the *actus reus* of obtaining services by deception is the obtaining by deception (see above) of services (the conferring of a benefit on the understanding that it will be paid for—whether the payment is legally enforceable or not). The *mens rea* is intention or subjective recklessness as to the deception, and "Ghosh" dishonesty.

What is "evading a liability by deception"?

Under TA '78, s.2, the *actus reus* of evading a liability by deception is the evasion (*i.e.* securing full or partial remission of an existing liability to make payment, inducing the creditor to wait or forego payment, or obtaining exemption from/abatement of a liability to make payment) of a legally enforceable liability by deception (see above). The *mens rea* is intention or subjective recklessness as to the deception, "Ghosh" dishonesty, and (regarding 'wait or forego' *only*) an intention to make permanent default.

How satisfactory are these deception offences?

The main criticism of the present law is that it is unnecessarily complex and difficult for prosecutors, judges, and juries to apply. The Law Commission 2002 Report on Fraud recommends replacing the existing offences with just two new ones:

(1) Fraud—where a person dishonestly: (a) makes a false representation; (b) wrongfully fails to disclose information; or (c) secretly abuses a position of trust, with intent to make a gain or cause loss or expose another to the risk of loss.
(2) Obtaining services dishonestly—where a person obtains services by any dishonest act with an intention to avoid payment. By removing any need for a deception, this is intended to be a 'theft-like' offence.

The Commission views the **benefits** of this change as being:

☑ A dramatic simplification of the law.
☑ It would be much easier for prosecutors, judges, and juries to apply.
☑ A single, comprehensive fraud offence would be better placed to deal with new, ingenious, and often technologically-based fraud.

What is "making off without payment"?

Under TA '78, s.3, the *actus reus* of making of without payment is making off (leaving the place at which payment is required or expected—*R v Brooks & Brooks* [1982]) without payment for goods supplied/services done where payment on the spot is required/expected (*R v Vincent* [2001]). The *mens rea* is knowledge that payment on the spot is required/expected, "Ghosh" dishonesty, and an intention to permanently avoid payment (*R v Allen* [1985]).

What is "criminal damage"?

Under the Criminal Damage Act 1971, s.1(1), the *actus reus* of criminal damage is to destroy or damage (cause physical harm, impairment, or deterioration that requires expense or more than minimal effort to rectify—*A (a juvenile) v R* [1978]; *Hardman v CC of Avon & Somerset* [1986]; *Morphitis v Salmon* [1990]) property (all tangible property, including land) belonging to another (see above), without lawful excuse (D will have lawful excuse where: (a) he honestly believes that the person he believes to be entitled to consent would have consented to the damage had they known of it and its circumstances; (b) the damage was done in order to protect property belonging to D or another where D honestly believed that the property was in immediate need of protection and the means adopted were reasonable in the circumstances). The *mens rea* is intention or subjective recklessness (*R v G and another* [2003]).

Under CDA, s.1(2), aggravated criminal damage is where D, in addition to intending or being subjectively reckless as to the damage (including damage to D's own property), also thereby intends or is subjectively reckless as to endangering the life of another. Under s.1(3), either criminal damage or aggravated criminal damage caused by fire is charged as arson where D either intends or is subjectively reckless as to damage by fire.

20. CRIMINAL LAW: PRELIMINARY OFFENCES AND PARTICIPATION

What are "preliminary offences"?

Preliminary (or inchoate) offences—**attempts**, **conspiracy**, and **incitement**—are concerned with the preparation or instigation of criminal acts. Their importance is that they enable early effective intervention prior to the commission of the full offence.

What are the elements of a criminal attempt?

Under the Criminal Attempts Act 1981, s.1, the *actus reus* of attempt is an act that is more than merely preparatory to the commission of the offence. The *mens rea* is an **intention** to commit the full offence.

What does "more than merely preparatory" mean?

While it is necessary to criminalise attempts, it would be neither sensible nor desirable to criminalise mere wicked thoughts or criminal fantasies. To attract liability, something must have been *done* to put those thoughts into effect. What this must be is open to a spectrum of possibilities, ranging from *any act* in a series of acts which, if completed, would constitute the full offence (Stephen's Digest [1894]), through to the *last act* required prior to the commission of the full offence (*R v Eagleton* [1855]; *DPP v Stonehouse* [1977]). According to the Court of Appeal in *R v Gullefer* [1990], the 1981 Act steers a middle course between these two extremes, observing that D must have gone beyond mere preparation and embarked upon the crime proper.

Is this a satisfactory definition?

While it avoids the excessive broadness of the 'any act' approach, the "Gullefer" approach can be criticised as being too close to the "last act" theory, and is thus *too narrow* to enable effective intervention at an early stage in the criminal enterprise (contrast, for example, *R v Jones* [1990] with *R v Campbell* [1991]). It is also rather vague and unpredictable in its application by juries (contrast, for example, *R v Geddes* [1996] with *R v Tosti* [1997]). However, it should be noted that the Law Commission report that preceded the Act observed that there was no "magic formula" and that some uncertainty was therefore inevitable.

Can it be a crime to attempt the impossible?

The Act makes it clear that a person *can* be convicted of an attempt in circumstances where the facts are such that commission of the full offence is impossible. Strangely, the House of Lords held this not to be the case in *Anderton v Ryan* [1985], but rapidly reversed this error by using the 1966 Practice Statement in *R v Shivpuri* [1986]. This only applies to factual impossibility, not legal impossibility—it is not an offence to attempt an act that is not itself a crime, even where D mistakenly believes that it is (*R v Taafe* [1983]).

What is "incitement"?

Incitement is a common law offence, and means to instigate a crime through advice, encouragement, persuasion, or compulsion. The *actus reus* is the act of incitement (whether written, spoken, or by conduct, and whether explicit or implicit—*Invicta Plastics v Clare* [1976]), and will be an offence even if the full offence is factually impossible (*R v McDonough* [1962]), though not where it is legally impossible (*R v Whitehouse* [1977]). The *mens rea* is an *intention* that the offence incited will be committed.

Do we need incitement?

While there is some overlap with other offences—for example, if the person incited agrees to commit the offence, there may be a criminal conspiracy—and if the offence incited is committed, the inciter may be liable as a secondary party (see below), there are still circumstances where this is not the case, and only incitement would enable effective early intervention. Therefore, it seems incitement is a necessary element in the rather untidy patchwork of inchoate and secondary offences.

What is a criminal conspiracy?

Under the Criminal Law Act 1977, s.1, a criminal conspiracy is an agreement between two or more persons (unless the only other person is the intended victim, D's spouse, or under 10 years of age) which, if carried out, would result in the commission of a crime by at least one of them. The *actus reus* is the fact of *agreement*. It is sufficient that D reaches agreement with at least one other conspirator (allowing for 'wheel' and 'chain' conspiracies). It is an offence to conspire at the factually impossible, but not the legally impossible. The *mens rea* is an *intention* that the agreement be carried out and that an offence be committed by at least one of the conspirators (*R v Edwards* [1991]).

Do we need conspiracy?

It both allows earlier intervention than is possible under the law on attempt, and brings the "criminal mastermind" within the scope of liability where they might otherwise be insulated against liability under the law on incitement or secondary participation. Therefore, as with incitement, conspiracy is a necessary element in the patchwork of inchoate and secondary offences.

What are "principal" and "secondary" offenders?

A **principal** offender is the person who **commits** the *actus reus*
of an offence. Under the Accessories and Abettors Act 1861, s.8,
a **secondary** offender is anyone who **aids**, **abets**, **counsels**, or
procures the commission of an indictable offence. Therefore, the
actus reus of secondary participation is:

> ➤ **Aiding**—the provision of material assistance at the time
> the offence is committed.
> ➤ **Abetting**—the provision of encouragement or advice at
> the time the offence is committed.
> ➤ **Counselling**—the provision of assistance, encouragement,
> or advice prior to the commission of the offence.
> ➤ **Procuring**—the commission of an act that causes or brings
> about the commission of an offence by another. It is not
> necessary to show that the other person was aware of D's
> conduct (*Attorney-General's Reference No.1* [1975]).

The *mens rea* is an intention to do the acts D knows are capable
of aiding, abetting, counselling or procuring the offence. It is not
necessary to show D intended the commission of the full offence
(*DPP for Northern Ireland v Lynch* [1975]; *R v JF Alford Transport*
[1997]).

What is a "joint enterprise"?

Where D is aiding or abetting the principal in the commission of
an offence, they are engaged on a joint enterprise, and D will be
liable as a secondary party to *any* offence falling within their
common purpose, but *not* to those that are fundamentally
different or were outside the range of offences contemplated by
D (*R v Powell and English* [1997]; *R v Uddin* [1998]; *R v Greatrex*
[1999]). D can avoid liability, however, by clearly and une-
quivocally withdrawing from the enterprise and by doing all
that is reasonably possible to neutralise any assistance, advice,
or encouragement already given (*R v Rook* [1993]).

Is the law on secondary participation satisfactory?

A Law Commission consultation paper (1993) proposed replacing the present complex and archaic law with two new
offences—assisting or encouraging the commission of crime.

These would be preliminary offences, removing the present requirement that the principal offence actually be committed, and would therefore be consistent with the law on attempts, incitement, and conspiracy. However, it may be that these two new offences would not cover the full range of conduct dealt with under the present law (see, for example, procuring). Other modern statutes use the terms "causing or encouraging" and "assisting and inducing". Therefore, in addition to assisting or encouraging, it may be necessary to add a third offence of causing (inducing) the commission of crime.

---

21. CONTRACT LAW: FORMATION OF CONTRACT

What is a "contract"?

A contract is a legally enforceable agreement. An agreement will amount to a contract where *five* characteristics are present: offer, acceptance, consideration, intention, and capacity.

What is an "offer"?

An offer is a proposition put by one person to another. This can be done orally, in writing, or by conduct, and can be made to a particular individual, group, or the world at large. To amount to an offer, it must be clear, precise, and capable of acceptance as it stands (*Harvey v Facey* [1893]; *Gibson v Manchester CC* [1979]). Offers must be distinguished from invitations to treat (an indication of a willingness to consider offers or enter negotiations). Common forms of invitation to treat are:

(1) Displays of goods for sale, whether in-store (*Pharmaceutical Society of GB v Boots* [1952]) or in a shop window (*Fisher v Bell* [1961]).
(2) Advertisements (*Partridge v Crittenden* [1968]).
(3) Auctions (*Sale of Goods Act 1979, s.57*), unless advertised as 'without reserve' (*Warlow v Harrison* [1859]; *Barry v Davies* [2000]).
(4) Tenders (*Spencer v Harding* [1870]), unless stated that lowest tender will be accepted (*Harvela Investments v Royal Trust of Canada* [1985]). Also, an invitation to tender may

be binding to extent that all properly submitted bids must be considered (*Blackpool & Fylde Aero Club v Blackpool BC* [1990]).

What happens to an offer if it isn't accepted?

If an offer is not accepted (see below), it will be terminated due to:

(1) **Revocation**—an offer may be revoked/withdrawn at any time prior to acceptance, unless an option has been purchased under a separate contract (*Payne v Cave* [1789]; *Routledge v Grant* [1828]). The revocation must be communicated to the offeree (the postal rule—see below—does *not* apply (*Byrne v Van Tienhoven* [1880])) by the offeror or a reliable third party (*Dickinson v Dodds* [1876]).

(2) **Rejection**—this immediately terminates the offer (*Hyde v Wrench* [1840]), and includes counter-offers (which seek to amend the original offer) but not mere requests for further details (*Stevenson, Jacques & Co v McLean* [1880]).

(3) **Lapse of time**—either once an express time limit has expired or after a reasonable time (*Ramsgate Victoria Hotel v Montefiore* [1866]).

(4) **Failure of condition** (*Financings Ltd v Stimson* [1962]).

(5) **Death of one of the parties**—death of the offeree terminates the offer. Death of the offeror will terminate the offer if the offeree has notice (*Re Whelan [1897]*)—otherwise it is only terminated where it could not be fulfilled by the offeror's personal representatives (*Bradbury v Morgan* [1862]).

What is "acceptance"?

To be effective, acceptance must exactly match the terms of the offer and be communicated to the offeror (*i.e.* actually brought to his notice—*Entores v Miles Far East Corp* [1955]). Any specified method of acceptance must be complied with (*Tinn v Hoffman* [1873]), but regarding preferred methods, any method no less advantageous to the offeror will be effective (*Manchester DCE v Commercial and General* [1969]).

The *postal rule* is an exception to this general rule—acceptance by post is effective as soon as it is posted (*Adams v Lindsell* [1818]), even if the letter is lost or delayed (*Household Insurance v*

Grant [1879]) provided it was properly addressed and stamped (*Re London and Northern Bank, ex parte Jones* [1900]). However, the rule only applies where postal acceptance is specified or is reasonable in the circumstances, and can be expressly excluded by the terms of the offer (*Holwell Securities v Hughes* [1974]). The rule also applies to analogous forms of non-instantaneous communication but not to written communication transmitted instantaneously (*Brinkibon v Stahag* [1983]). Regarding e-commerce, the display of goods on the website and the buyer's initial response are invitations to treat, the seller's communication of the order details is an offer, and the buyer's confirmation is acceptance (Electronic Commerce (EC Directive) Regulations 2002).

What is "consideration"?

Consideration transforms the agreement (offer + acceptance) into a bargain. It is what one person does or promises to do in return for the act or promise of the other. To be valid, consideration must:

(1) Be either a detriment to the promise or a benefit to the promisor.
(2) Move from the promise but need not move to the promisor—*i.e.* it can move to a third party (*Tweddle v Atkinson* [1861]). Under the doctrine of *privity of contract*, that third party could not enforce the agreement as they were not a party to the contract. However, under the Contracts (Rights of Third Parties) Act 1999, a third party may bring a claim where the contract expressly provides for this or the contract purports to confer a benefit on them (unless it is clear from the contract that the main parties did not intend it to be enforceable by the third party).
(3) Be sufficient (*i.e.* something of value) but need not be adequate (*i.e.* have parity of value)—the law is concerned with the existence of the bargain, not its quality (*Thomas v Thomas* [1842]; *Chappell v Nestle* [1960]).
(4) Not be past—past consideration is no consideration (*Roscorla v Thomas* [1952]; *Re McArdle [1951]*).

Performance of an *existing duty* will be valid consideration where it arises from a contract with a different party (*Scotson v*

Pegg [1861]; *New Zealand Shipping v Satterthwaite* [1975]). However, where the duty arises under the general law (*Collins v Godefroy* [1831]; *Glasbrook v Glamorgan CC* [1925]), or under an earlier contract with the same party (*Stilk v Myrick* [1809]; *Hartley v Ponsonby* [1857]), then it will only be valid where that performance **exceeds** that required by the existing duty. However, mere re-affirmation of an earlier promise may be valid consideration where it is of benefit to the promise, provided the later agreement was not procured by fraud or economic duress (*Williams v Roffey* [1991]).

Regarding debts, the *Rule in Pinnel's Case* [1602] states that part-payment cannot be valid consideration for a promise to forego the remainder. However, the rule does *not* apply where:

(1) Part-payment was made before the due date at the creditor's request.
(2) Part-payment was made at different place at the creditor's request.
(3) Part-payment accompanied by goods, or settlement by goods alone, is made at the creditor's request.
(4) The amount owed is disputed.
(5) The smaller sum is paid by a third party (*Hirachand Punamchand v Temple* [1911]).
(6) The debtor has entered into a "composition agreement" with his creditors.

Furthermore, under the equitable doctrine of *promissory estoppel*, the court may prevent the creditor going back on his promise to accept a lesser sum where the debtor has relied on that promise and it would be inequitable to allow the creditor to recant (*Central London Property v High Trees House* [1947]).

What is "intention"?

The parties must intend their agreement to be legally binding. In deciding this, the law uses *two* presumptions:

(1) **Social and domestic agreements** are presumed *not* to be legally binding (*Balfour v Balfour* [1919]) unless there is clear evidence to the contrary (*Merritt v Merritt* [1970])
(2) **Business and commercial agreements** are presumed to be legally binding unless there is clear evidence to the contrary (*e.g.* the use of an 'honour' clause—*Rose and Frank v Crompton* [1923]).

What is "capacity"?

While most people have full contractual capacity (the ability to make contracts), the law restricts the capacity of *three* groups to protect them from exploitation:

(1) If someone with a **mental disorder** that prevents them from understanding the nature or significance of a contract, makes a contract and the other party was or ought to have been aware of that disorder, then the contract will be voidable (*Molton v Camroux* [1848]). However, where the contract is one for "necessaries", then the contract is binding to the extent that the disordered party may be required to pay a reasonable sum (*Re Rhodes* [1890]; Sale of Goods Act 1979, s.3).

(2) **Drunkards** are in the same position as the mentally disordered (*Gore v Gibson* [1845]; Sale of Goods Act 1979, s.3).

(3) A **minor** is bound by contracts for necessary goods and services to the extent of being required to pay a reasonable price for them (*Chapple v Cooper* [1844]; *Nash v Inman* [1908]; Sale of Goods Act 1979, s.3). Minors are also bound by beneficial contracts of service, such as apprenticeships (*Doyle v White City Stadium* [1935]). Contracts concerning land, shares, or partnerships made by a minor are voidable. Contracts for non-necessaries and contracts of loan made by a minor are void. However, under the Minors' Contracts Act 1987, any guarantee of a loan to a minor given by an adult *is* enforceable, and the courts may order the return of any non-necessary goods (or their proceeds of sale).

22. CONTRACT LAW: VITIATING FACTORS

What are "vitiating factors"?

These are factors that either destroy (make void) or undermine (make voidable) an apparently valid contract. Where the contract is *void*, the parties must be returned to their pre-contractual position, a process known as **restitution**. Where the contract is *voidable*, the party seeking to avoid it will apply for **rescission**, again returning them to their pre-contractual position. Rescission is a discretionary, equitable remedy, and will *not* be granted where: (a) the contract has been affirmed; (b) substantial restitution is not possible; (c) a third party has acquired rights in the subject-matter in good faith and for value.

What is "lack of form"?

While most contracts are "simple" contracts (*i.e.* there are no formal requirements), some (*e.g.* those concerning land) must be in writing or evidenced in writing in order to be valid.

What is "duress and undue influence"?

Duress (whether physical or economic—*Universe Tankships v ITWF* [1983]) and undue influence (the abuse of a privileged position of influence) make a contract voidable.

What is "illegality" and "public policy"?

A contract is void if it is illegal in either its object (*e.g.* a contract to commit a crime) or its manner of performance (*e.g.* unlicensed trading). Contrary to the general position, any money/goods exchanged are *not* recoverable (*Parkinson v College of Ambulance* [1925]).

What is "mistake"?

There are *three* situations where a mistake by one of the parties will make the contract void:

(1) Mistake as to the nature of the subject-matter (but not mistake as to its quality) (*Raffles v Wichelhaus* [1864]).
(2) Mistake as to the existence of the subject-matter (*Strickland v Turner* [1852]).
(3) Mistake as to the identity of the other party, but *only* where the *precise* identity of the that party is crucial to the other's decision to enter the contract (*Cundy v Lindsay* [1878]; *Shogun Finance v Hudson* [2004]).

What is "misrepresentation"?

A misrepresentation is an untrue statement made during pre-contractual negotiations. Whether it is an operative misrepresentation, and the consequences if it is, depend upon the:

(1) **Nature of the statement**—it must be a statement of fact (not law, opinion, or intention. Generally, remaining silent cannot amount to a misrepresentation (*Fletcher v Krell* [1873]) except where: (a) it is a failure to notify a change in material circumstances (*With v O'Flanagan* [1936]); (b) it is a "half-truth", therby creating a false impression (*Nottingham Patent Brick and Tile Co v Butler* [1886]); the contract is one of utmost good faith (*e.g.* insurance contracts).

(2) **Nature of the inducement**—the misrepresentee must have relied on the truth of the statement in deciding to enter the contract (*Attwood v Small* [1838]; *Redgrave v Hurd* [1881]), though it need not be the sole factor in the decision (*Edgington v Fitzmaurice* [1885]).

(3) **Nature of the misrepresentation**—an operative misrepresentation makes the contract voidable. If it is fraudulent, the innocent party can also claim damages in the tort of deceit. If it is negligent, they can also claim damages under the Misrepresentation Act 1967. If it is innocent, they can claim damages in lieu of rescission under the Misrepresentation Act 1967.

---

23. CONTRACT LAW: TERMS OF THE CONTRACT

What are "contractual terms"?

It is the terms of the contract that identify the rights and duties of the parties. Contractual terms can be classified in *two* ways:

(1) By their **status** or importance. *Conditions* are the most important or central terms, while *warranties* are the less important or peripheral terms. *Innominate terms* are those whose importance is unclear, and this is determined in light of any breach. The importance of distinguishing between terms in this way relates to the consequences that flow from their breach (see Chapter 24).

(2) By their **origin**. *Express* terms are those actually stated by the parties themselves. *Implied* terms are those that are incorporated into the contract by common law or statute

(*e.g.* Sale of Goods Act 1979). The courts will only imply a term at common law where it is not only reasonable, but also obvious and necessary to give business efficacy to the contract (*The Moorcock* [1889]; *Liverpool CC v Irwin* [1977])—*e.g.* where such a term is commercial custom and practice (*Hutton v Warren* [1836]).

---

24. CONTRACT LAW: DISCHARGE OF CONTRACT

How can a contract end?

A contract can end in *four* ways: performance, agreement, frustration, and breach.

What is "performance"?

A contract comes to an end when the parties have performed their obligations under it. Generally, performance must be exact and entire, except where:

(1) The contract can be sub-divided into smaller, identical contracts (*i.e.* is a severable contract), where the party in breach may nevertheless claim for those elements performed (*Ritchie v Atkinson* [1808]; *Atkinson v Ritchie* [1809]).

(2) The party in breach was prevented from performing their obligations by the other party (*Planche v Colburn* [1831]).

(3) Where the other party had a genuine choice to accept partial performance and did so (*Sumpter v Hedges* [1898]).

(4) Where one party has substantially performed their obligations, subject to only a minor defect, they may enforce the contract subject to a reduction to compensate for the defect (*Hoenig v Isaacs* [1952]; *Bolton v Mahadeva* [1972]).

(5) Where one party tenders/offers performance (other than payment of a debt) and the other party rejects it.

What is "agreement"?

Just as the contract was created by agreement, it may be ended by agreement. As with the original agreement, this must be supported by fresh consideration.

What is "frustration"?

Frustration is where **further performance** of the contract is either **impossible** (*Taylor v Caldwell* [1863]; *Jackson v Union Marine Insurance* [1874]; *Morgan v Manser* [1948]), **illegal** (the *Fibrosa* case [1943]), or **radically different** from that anticipated by both parties when the contract was made (*Krell v Henry* [1903]; *Herne Bay Steamboat Co v Hutton* [1903]; *Davis Contractors v Fareham UDC* [1956]), and the frustrating event was not due to the fault of either party (*Maritime National Fish v Ocean Trawlers* [1935]). Under the Law Reform (Frustrated Contracts) Act 1943, the consequences of frustration are:

(1) The contract is immediately discharged and the parties released from any further obligations.
(2) Money paid can be recovered.
(3) Money due but not in fact paid ceases to be payable.
(4) Expenses incurred can be recovered up to the limit of any sums paid/due to be paid.
(5) A party that has acquired a valuable benefit can be required to pay a reasonable sum for it.

What is "breach"?

A breach of contract occurs where one party fails to perform some or all of their obligations (*actual breach*), or gives a clear indication of an intention to do so (*anticipatory breach*—which gives rise to an immediate right to sue—*Hochster v De la Tour* [1853]). A breach of condition (*repudiatory breach*) gives the injured party a right to damages (see chapter 25) and the option to repudiate (regard as discharged) the contract. Breach of warranty (*mere breach*) gives rise to a right to damages only, and does *not* discharge the contract. Breach of an innominate term will be regarded as breach of condition where it substantially deprives the injured party of their anticipated contractual benefits, and as a breach of warranty where it has only minor consequences (*The Hansa Nord* [1976]).

25. CONTRACT LAW: REMEDIES

What are "damages"?

Damages are financial compensation for a legal wrong. In contract, the aim is to put the injured party in their anticipated post-contractual position (*Robinson v Harman* [1848]). A claim for damages can take *two* forms:

(1) **Liquidated damages**—this is where the contract specifies the amount to paid (or a formula for working it out) in the event of a particular breach. These are valid where they are a genuine attempt to estimate the likely loss, but not where they are a penalty clause designed to compel performance (*Dunlop v New Garage* [1915]). It will be regarded as a penalty clause where: (a) the specified sum is greater than any conceivable loss; (b) the breach is a failure to pay sums due and the damages specified exceed that sum; (c) the same sum is specified for both major and minor breaches.

(2) **Unliquidated damages**—this is a claim based on the actual loss suffered. The injured party may claim for: (a) losses (including consequential losses) that are a natural consequence of the breach; and (b) other losses that were known to be a possibility by both parties at the time the contract was made (*Hadley v Baxendale* [1854]; *The Heron II* [1969]).

The court is entitled to engage in a degree of *speculation* in calculating the actual loss (*e.g.* loss of a chance—*Chaplin v Hicks* [1911]). Also, the injured party is required to take all reasonable steps to *mitigate* (keep to a minimum) their losses (*British Westinghouse v Underground Electric Railways* [1912]).

What is "specific performance"?

This is a discretionary, equitable remedy that requires the party in breach to perform their obligations. It is rarely awarded (except in land transactions), and will not be awarded where:

(1) Damages are adequate (*Cohen v Roche* [1927]).
(2) The remedy would not be available to both parties (*e.g.* contracts with minors—*Flight v Bolland* [1828]).

(3) It would require constant supervision (*Ryan v Mutual Tontine* [1893]).
(4) The contract is for personal services (*Rigby v Connol* [1880]).

What are "injunctions"?

A prohibitory injunction may be awarded to prevent breach of an express negative obligation (*e.g.* a valid restraint of trade clause—*Lumley v Wagner* [1852]; *Warner Bros v Nelson* [1937]), but *not* where to do so would compel performance of other, positive obligations for which specific performance would not be granted (*Page One Records v Britton* [1967]).

26. CONTRACT LAW: CONSUMER CONTRACTS

What are the rules regarding sale of goods?

These are found in the Sale of Goods Act 1979 (as amended by the Sale and Supply of Goods Act 1994). A contract for the sale of goods is one where the ownership of goods is exchanged for money (s.2). There are *four* important **implied terms** in the Act:

(1) The seller has the right to sell the goods (s.12).
(2) Where the sale is a sale by description, the goods must *correspond with that description* (s.13).
(3) Where the seller is selling in the course of a business, the goods must be of *satisfactory quality* (s.14). This applies to all goods (including 'seconds' and 'second-hand') and covers both functional and cosmetic characteristics. However, this does *not* apply to: (a) defects drawn to the buyer's attention before the contract was made; (b) defects that a reasonable examination would have revealed, provided the buyer in fact examined the goods before the contract was made. Also, the general requirement is that goods are fit for their common purpose, and the goods only need to be fit for a particular purpose (other than the

common purpose) where: (a) the buyer made that purpose known to the seller; (b) the buyer relied on the seller's skill and judgement; and (c) that reliance was not unreasonable in the circumstances.

(4) Where the sale is a sale by sample, the bulk of the goods will *correspond to the sample* in quality (s.15).

As these are implied 'conditions', then any breach will *prima facie* be a repudiatory breach. However, the right to repudiate will be lost if the seller has 'accepted' the goods by (s.35):

(1) Indicating acceptance to the seller.
(2) Doing something with/to the goods that is inconsistent with the ownership of the seller. This does *not* include testing the goods to ensure that they conform to the contract. Also, agreeing to the repair of faulty goods does not amount to acceptance—if they are still unsatisfactory following repair, the buyer may still reject them.
(3) Keeping the goods beyond a reasonable time without indicating any intention to reject them to the seller.

What are the rules regarding supply of goods and services?

These are found in the Supply of Goods and Services Act 1982 (as amended by the Sale and Supply of Goods Act 1994). The Act applies to contracts for the:

(1) **Transfer of goods** (where ownership is exchanged for something other than money), and implies similar terms to those in the 1979 Act.
(2) **Hire of goods** (where possession is transferred for a specific time), and implies similar terms to those in the 1979 Act.
(3) **Supply of a service**, where the Act implies terms that: (a) the service will be carried out with reasonable care and skill (s.13); (b) that unless specifically provided for in the contract, the service will be carried out within a reasonable time; (c) that unless specifically provided for in the contract, a reasonable price will be paid for the service.

What are "exclusion clauses"?

These are contractual terms that seek to exclude or limit liability for breach of contract. While legitimate in principle, they can be misused by parties in a dominant bargaining position, particularly when included in "standard form contracts". Therefore, they are regulated both by the courts and by statute:

(1) **Judicial regulation** takes two forms: (a) the clause must have been properly *incorporated* into the contract—*i.e.* the other party must have been given reasonably sufficient notice of the clause (*Parker v SE Railway* [1877]) at or before the time the contract was made (*Olley v Marlborough Court* [1949]; *Thornton v Shoe Lane Parking* [1971]); (b) upon proper *construction*, the clause must cover the breach that has occurred—the benefit of any doubt is given to the injured party (*Baldry v Marshall* [1925]; *Andrews v Singer* [1934]; *L'Estrange v Graucob* [1934]), and it is presumed that the clause was not intended to defeat the main purpose of the contract (*Glynn v Margetson* [1893]) unless there are sufficiently strong and clear words to the contrary (*Suisse Atlantique* [1967]; *Photo Production v Securicor* [1980]).

(2) **Statutory regulation** under the Unfair Contract Terms Act 1977 provides that: (a) business liability (whether contractual or tortuous) for causing death or personal injury through negligence (including breach of SOGSA, s.13) cannot be excluded or restricted; (b) negligence liability for other loss/damage can only be excluded/restricted insofar as the term is reasonable; (c) liability for breach of SOGA, s.12, cannot be excluded/restricted; (d) liability for breach of SOGA, ss.13–15 cannot be excluded against a consumer, and only as against a non-consumer insofar as the term is reasonable; (e) similar limitations apply as regards the implied terms in SOGSA relating to the transfer/hire of goods. A consumer is someone who is not dealing in the course of a business contracting with someone who is, and, with regard to goods, the goods must be of a type ordinarily supplied for private use or consumption. Also of relevance here are the Unfair Terms in Consumer Contracts Regulations 1999, which regulate the use of standard form contracts. These provide that: (a) any term deemed unfair will not be binding on the consumer; (b) a term is unfair if it causes a significant imbalance in rights and obligations to the detriment of the

consumer; (c) contracts should be written in plain, intelligible language, and the benefit of any doubt will be given to the consumer.

---

27. CONTRACT LAW: CONSUMER PROTECTION

What are "trade descriptions"?

A trade description is a description applied in the course of a trade or business, including both primary and incidental trading activities (*Havering LBC v Stevenson* [1970]; *Davies v Sumner* [1984]). These are regulated by the Trade Descriptions Act 1968, which creates two criminal offences (s.1): (a) applying a false trade description to goods; (b) supplying/offering to supply goods to which a false trade description has been applied.

A trade description is any indication, however given, of (s.2): quantity, size, or gauge; method of manufacture or processing; composition; physical characteristics; testing or approval by any person; place of manufacture; person by whom manufactured; other history, including previous ownership or use. A trade description is false if it is false or misleading to a material degree (s.3). A trade description is applied if it is fixed, marked on, or attached to the goods or their packaging, or is made in any manner that could be taken as applying to the goods (s.4), including any advertisement (s.5), catalogue, circular or price list (s.39). A person offers goods for supply (contrary to the usual rules on invitations to treat) if they expose them for supply or have them in their possession for supply (s.6). The supplier need only know that the description has been applied, he need not know that it is false (*Cottee v Douglas Seaton (Used Cars) Ltd* [1972]).

Regarding services, s.14 makes it an offence for any person in the course of business or trade to knowingly or recklessly make a false statement regarding: the provision or nature of any services, accommodation, or facilities; the time at which or the person by whom they will be provided; the examination, approval, or evaluation by any person of such services, accommodation, or facilities; the location or amenities of any accommodation. A person charged with supplying/offering to supply may have a defence where: (a) a clear and compelling disclaimer has been used; (b) the offence is due to mistake, reliance on information supplied by another, the act or default of another, or an accident AND they have taken all reasonable precautions and exercised all due diligence to avoid the commission of an offence; (c) they did not know, and could not with due diligence have discovered that either the description had been applied or that it was false (s.24). An advertiser may have a defence where the advertisement was received and published in the course of a business involving such publication, and they did not know and had no reason to know that the publication would amount to an offence (s.25).

What are the rules on price indications?

These are found in Part III of the Consumer Protection Act 1987. It is an offence for any person, in the course of business, to give to consumers by any means whatsoever a misleading price indication regarding goods, services, accommodation, or facilities (s.20). A price indication is misleading where it indicates that: (a) the price is less than it is; (b) that the price does not depend on facts or circumstances on which it does depend; (c) that it covers matters for which an additional charge is made (d) that someone who has no such expectation, expects the price to be increased, reduced, or maintained; (e) that the facts or circumstances by which a consumer might judge the validity of any comparison made or implied are not what they are (s.21). A due diligence defence is provided by s.39.

What if the product is dangerous?

Where a product is dangerous, the purchaser can bring a claim for breach of contract, while a non-purchaser may have a claim in negligence. Alternatively, either may bring a claim under Part I of the Consumer Protection Act 1987. The Act creates a regime of strict liability for damage caused wholly or in part by defective products (s.2). It covers death, personal injury, and damage to private property (*i.e.* property of a type ordinarily intended for private use, occupation, or consumption), excluding damage to the product itself and claims of less than £275. "Product" excludes game and agricultural produce that has not undergone an industrial process. A product is "defective" if it is not reasonably safe (s.3)—relevant factors include: (a) the manner in which and purposes for which it has been marketed; (b) what might reasonably be expected to be done with or to it; (c) any instructions or warnings supplied with it; (d) the time at which it was supplied (the 'state of the art' factor). An action may be brought against: (a) the producer; (b) any person who by putting his name or trade mark on the product, has held himself out as the producer; (c) any person who has imported the product into the EU in the course of a business; (d) the supplier, but only where they have failed to comply with a reasonable request to identify (a)-(c) (s.2). The Act provides for a number of specific defences: (a) the defect is due to compliance with a legal requirement; (b) the person had not supplied it to another; (c) the supply was not in the course of a business or with a view to profit; (d) the defect did not exist at the time of supply; (e) the state of scientific and technical knowledge at the relevant time was not such that the producer might have been expected to discover the defect (the "development risks" defence); (f) the defect was in a subsequent product in which the product in question had been incorporated (*i.e.* was a component) and was wholly attributable to the design of the subsequent product or compliance with instructions given by the producer of the subsequent product.

How are these measures enforced?

The main enforcement agencies for consumer protection legislation are local authority Trading Standards and Environmental Health Departments. The government department with overall responsibility for consumer issues is the Department of Trade and Industry.

---

28. TORT: NEGLIGENCE

What is "negligence"?

Negligence is the failure to take reasonable care where a duty to do so exists, and where that breach of duty causes reasonably foreseeable recoverable loss or damage to the person to whom the duty is owed. Thus, there are *five* elements: (a) recoverable loss; (b) duty of care; (c) breach of duty; (d) causing loss or damage; (e) the foreseeability of that loss or damage.

What damage is recoverable?

Personal injury, damage to property, and economic loss consequential on either of these, are all recoverable forms of damage or loss. Generally, however, pure economic loss is *not* recoverable (*Spartan Steel v Martin* [1973]; *D & F Estates v Church Commissioners* [1989]; *Murphy v Brentwood DC* [1990]), unless there was a "special relationship" where the claimant was relying on the specialist skill and knowledge of the defendant (*Hedley Byrne v Heller* [1964]; *Junior Books v Veitchi* [1982]; *Simaan v Pilkington* [1988]).

When does a "duty of care" arise?

The basis of a duty of care is the principle of "**neighbourhood**" developed by Lord Atkin in *Dononoghue v Stevenson* [1932]: (a) a person is under a duty of care to avoid acts or omissions that they could reasonably foresee might injure their neighbour; (b) a neighbour is someone so closely and directly affected by their acts or omissions that they ought reasonably to have them in contemplation as being so affected when directing their mind to the acts or omission that are called in question. This "neigbourhood" test has since been modified into the present test of "proximity"—that there must be a sufficiently close relationship between the claimant and the defendant that it is fair, just, and reasonable in the circumstances to impose a duty of care (*Caparo v Dickman* [1990]; *Davis v Radcliffe* [1990]). While proximity cannot exist without neighbourhood, there are situations where the courts have imposed additional requirements over and above neighbourhood in order to establish the necessary proximity—for example:

(1) **Negligent statements**—here a "special relationship" is required (*Hedley Byrne v Heller* [1964]), the requirements of which are that (*Caparo v Dickman* [1990]): (a) the person seeking advice was relying on the other to exercise reasonable care and skill in their reply; (b) such reliance was reasonable in the circumstances; (b) the other person knew their reply was in connection with a particular

transaction or transactions of a particular kind; (d) and knew that the statement would be relied on in deciding whether or not to enter that transaction or transactions of that kind. However, the maker of the statement need not be in the business of giving information or advice of the type sought, provided they held themselves out as possessing the required skill or knowledge and this was reasonably relied on (*Chaudhry v Prabhakar* [1988]).

(2) **Psychological injury**—a person is owed a duty of care in respect of psychological injury where; (a) it is consequent upon physical injury to themselves, or a reasonably apprehended fear of such injury (*Dulieu v White* [1901]); (b) personal injury to the claimant (whether physical or psychological) is reasonably foreseeable (*Page v Smith* [1995]). Also, a person is owed a duty of care in respect of psychological injury consequent on injury/fear of injury to another where (*Alcock v CC of South Yorkshire Police* [1991]): (a) the claimant sees/hears the accident or its immediate aftermath; (b) the claimant (the secondary victim) has a close relationship of love and affection with that other person (the primary victim) (*Mc Farlane v E E Caledonia* [1993]), or the claimant is a rescuer (*Chadwick v British Transport Commission* [1967]; (c) psychological injury to the secondary victim is reasonably foreseeable (*Page v Smith* [1995]). The "immediate aftermath" extends to any medical facility to which the primary victim is taken, and persists for so long as they are in the state produced by the accident (including immediate post-accident treatment) (*McLoughlin v O'Brian* [1982]).

What is a breach of duty?

A person is in breach of duty if they fail to show the degree of care that a reasonable person would have taken in the circumstances (*i.e.* it is an **objective** test). The reasonable person is expected to possess a certain amount of basic level and an ordinary level of skill. Expert knowledge or skill is generally not required, except where such knowledge or skill is claimed (*Phillips v William Whitely* [1938])—even then, the standard required is that of the reasonably competent expert. It may be evidence of reasonable care to show that the defendant acted in accordance with accepted practice at the material time, discounting subsequent advances (*Roe v Minister of Health* [1954]), unless it can be shown that such practice is itself negligent (*Cavanagh v Ulster Weaving Co* [1960]). There are also *four* situations where this objective standard will be modified to accommodate subjective characteristics of the defendant:

(1) Where the defendant has some physical or mental incapacity.
(2) Young people are not expected to show the same degree of care as adults (*Gough v Thorne* [1966]).
(3) Elderly people are not expected to show the same degree of mental or physical agility as a younger adult (*Daly v Liverpool Corporation* [1939]), though they are expected to take account of the effects of ageing.
(4) Sudden and incapacitating illness with no forewarning (*Ryan v Youngs* [1938]).

In establishing what level of care would amount to reasonable care in the circumstances, *two* factors are considered:

(1) The degree of risk created—the greater the risk, the greater the obligation to take care, although the risk may be so slight that it would be reasonable to discount it entirely (*Bolton v Stone* [1951]).
(2) The severity of the potential harm—the greater the potential harm, the greater the obligation to take care to prevent it (*Paris v Stepney BC* [1951]).

What is the "requirement of causation"?

As liability in negligence is fault-based, it must be shown that it was the defendant's breach of duty that caused the claimant's loss or damage. This is established by using a "but for" test—*i.e.* but for the defendant's breach of duty, the claimant's loss or damage would not have occurred (*Barnett v Chelsea & Kensington Hospital* [1969]; *Hotson v East Berks HA* [1987]; *Wilsher v Essex AHA* [1988]). Generally, the breach of duty must have made a significant material contribution to the loss/damage, though it need not be the sole cause (*Bonningtons Castings v Wardlaw* [1956])—materially increasing the risk of loss/damage is *not* sufficient (*Wilsher v Essex AHA* [1988]; *Page v Smith* (No.2) [1996]). However, where the loss or damage *must* have been caused by at least one of the defendants, each of whom has been in breach of duty, but it is not possible to demonstrate which actually caused the harm, then the claimant may succeed against all (*Fairchild v Glenhaven Funeral Services* [2002]).

What is meant by "foreseeability" and "remoteness"?

The claimant may only recover for loss or damage that was a *reasonably foreseeable consequence* of the defendant's breach of duty (*The Wagon Mound (No.1)* [1961]). All other losses are regarded as *too remote* from the breach, and hence not recoverable. However, the claimant does *not* have to show that the *precise* nature, extent, or manner of occurrence was foreseeable (*Stewart v West African Air Terminals* [1964]), but only that they suffered a reasonably foreseeable type of loss occurring in a reasonably foreseeable manner (*Hughes v Lord Advocate* [1963]; *Bradford v Robinson Rentals* [1967]; *Doughty v Turner Manufacturing* [1964]; *Jolley v Sutton LBC* [2000]). The extent of the damage does *not* have to be reasonably foreseeable (*Vacwell Engineering v BDH Chemicals* [1971]). Also, the "thin skull" rule requires the defendant to their victim as they find them, and they will remain fully liable for damage aggravated by either the physical (*Dulieu v White* [1901]; *Smith v Leech Brain* [1962]) or mental (*Brice v Brown* [1984]) peculiarities of the claimant.

What defences may be raised?

There are *three* main defences:

(1) **Contributory negligence**—this is where the claimant's damage was caused in part by their *own* negligence. Under the Law Reform (Contributory Negligence) Act 1945, this is a partial defence enabling the court to reduce the claimant's compensation in proportion to their contribution to it. The relative contribution of the claimant and defendant's negligence is assessed according to: (a) the extent to which they were a cause of the damage (the "**causative potency**" test); (b) the degree to which each departed from the required standard of care (the "**degree of blameworthiness**" test). Where contributory negligence is alleged against a worker, consideration may be given to the fact that their appreciation of risk may have lessened through familiarity with the work, or the noise and stress of the workplace (*Grant v Sun Shipping* [1948]). Also, where the claimant has been placed in a position of peril by the defendant's negligence, they will not be held

contributory negligent in deciding to attempt to escape that peril (*Jones v Boyce* [1816]; *Haynes v Harwood* [1935]), but may be held contributory negligent in the manner of its execution (*Sayers v Harlow UDC* [1958]).

(2) **Volenti non fit injuria**—this is where the claimant has consented to the risk of injury through the defendant's negligence, and acts as a full defence. However, this will only arise where the injury is a virtual certainty (*Owens v Brimnell* [1977]; *Ashton v Turner* [1981]) and four requirements are met (*ICI v Shatwell* [1965]): (a) the claimant was aware of the defendant's negligence; (b) the claimants was aware of the risk to themselves this created; (c) the claimant continued to participate freely in the activity in the face of this knowledge; (d) the damage suffered was a reasonably foreseeable consequence of the risk consented to.

(3) **Exclusion of liability**—the defendant may be able to rely on an express undertaking by the claimant to accept the risk of negligence. However, the extent to which this may be done in any business or commercial context is severely restricted by the Unfair Contract Terms Act 1977 (s.2): (a) liability for causing death or personal injury through negligence cannot be excluded or restricted by any contractual term or non-contractual notice; (b) liability for other forms of loss can only be excluded/restricted insofar as the term/notice in reasonable; (c) a person's consent to or awareness of any such term/notice does not, of itself, amount to *volenti*.

How are damages calculated?

The aim of damages is to compensate the claimant for the loss or damage suffered. This is relatively straightforward where the loss or damage caused is physical damage to property or economic loss (where recoverable). The position is more problematic in relation to compensation for personal injury. Here, damages may be awarded under two main heads:

(1) **non-pecuniary loss**—the claimant may recover for the injury itself and any associated pain and suffering and/or loss of amenity.

(2) **pecuniary loss**—any loss of earnings up to the date of trial must be specifically pleaded as 'special damages'. Loss of future earnings may only be claimed speculatively

as "general damages". Any claim for loss of future earnings may include an amount for the "lost years" due to a reduction in life expectancy (*Pickett v British Rail Engineering* [1980]).

Damages may be paid either as a one-off lump-sum or as a smaller lump-sum accompanied by an annuity or pension (*i.e.* a "structured settlement", the terms of which must be approved by the court).

29. TORT: OCCUPIERS' LIABILITY

The Occupiers' Liability Act 1957

This Act imposes a common duty of care on the occupiers of premises towards lawful visitors to those premises (s.2). This is a duty to take reasonable care to ensure the premises are reasonably safe, and extends to the visitor's physical safety in all circumstances, but only damage to property caused by structural defects (s.1). A higher degree of care is required towards child visitors, particularly in respect of any "allurements" on the premises (*Glasgow Corporation v Taylor* [1922]). A lower degree of care is required towards professional visitors in respect of risks or hazards incidental to their calling or profession (*Roles v Nathan* [1963]). "Lawful visitors" include invitees, licensees, contractual visitors, and statutory visitors, but not other common law visitors (*Greenhalgh v BRB* [1969]) or trespassers (*BRB v Herrington* [1972]), though these latter groups are owed a common law duty of humanity and may be protected under the 1984 Act. An "occupier" is anyone in control of the premises, and they need not have any legal or equitable interest in the property (*Wheat v Lacon* [1966]). "Premises" includes not only land and buildings, but also any fixed or moveable structure, including vehicles, vessels, and aircraft. The Act provides for a specific defence of "warnings"—where a clear warning is given that, if observed, would make the visitor safe, then the occupier will not be liable for any damage caused by the visitor's failure to observe that warning (*Rafcliff v McConnell* [1999]; *Tomlinson v Congleton BC* [2003]). An occupier may also, in appropriate circumstances, raise contributory negligence or volenti (see Chapter 28).

The Occupiers' Liability Act 1984

This Act imposes a limited duty of care on the occupiers of premises towards visitors other than lawful visitors. This is a duty to take reasonable care to prevent personal injury as a result of "specific dangers" on the premises. A danger is a "specific" danger where:

(1) The occupier is aware of the danger or has reasonable grounds to believe it exists.
(2) The occupier knows or has reasonable grounds to believe that the other person is/is likely to come into the vicinity of the danger.
(3) The danger is one against which, in all the circumstances, the occupier may reasonably be expected to offer protection.

30. TORT: NUISANCE

What is "private nuisance"?

Private nuisance is the indirect and unreasonable interference with the use or enjoyment of neighbouring land (*Sedleigh-Denfield v O'Callaghan* [1940]) through, for example, noise, smoke, odours, fumes, water and plant and tree roots. The basis of liability is the failure to meet the reasonable expectations of one's neighbours. Therefore, if the defendant's conduct in fact causes an actionable nuisance, it is no defence to show that he has taken reasonable care to prevent it. If the defendant cannot carry on a particular activity without causing a nuisance, then he should not carry it on or, at least, carry it on somewhere else (*Rapier v London Tramways Co* [1893]). A nuisance is only actionable where it causes damage to the claimant's interests. This is clearly satisfied where the nuisance causes physical damage to the claimant's land. Where the damage is disturbance to use or enjoyment, this must be more than trivial (*Andreae v*

Selfridge [1938]) as the law expects a degree of give-and-take between neighbours (*Bamford v Turnley* [1862]). Other relevant factors include:

(1) The nuisance must be of a continuing or regular nature. Isolated or irregular instances will not normally amount to a nuisance (*Bolton v Stone* [1951]), except where the defendant is responsible for a continuous state of affairs with the potential for nuisance (*Spicer v Smee* [1946]).

(2) Regarding disturbance to use or enjoyment, the court may consider the character of the neighbourhood (*St Helen's Smelting Co v Tipping* [1865]).

(3) The fact the claimant may be unusually sensitive is not relevant to liability (*Robinson v Kilvert* [1889]), though it may be relevant to remedies (*McKinnon Industries Ltd v Walker* [1951]).

(4) While malice is not an essential requirement, it may tip the balance, converting otherwise reasonable conduct into an actionable nuisance (*Christie v Davey* [1893]; *Hollywood Silver Fox Farm Ltd v Emmett* [1936]).

(5) The defendant may be liable for a nuisance caused by the fault of another or due to natural causes ("adoption" or "continuance" of nuisance), where they knew or ought to have known of the nuisance and failed to take reasonable steps to stop it (*Leakey v National Trust* [1980]).

The claimant must have a legal or equitable interest in the land affected (*Malone v Laskey* [1907]; *Hunter v Canary Wharf Ltd* [1997]). Regarding disturbance to use or enjoyment, the claimant must also be in actual possession of the land (*Cooper v Crabtree* [1882]).Where the damage is physical damage, a person with an interest out of possession (*e.g.* a landlord) may sue (*Colwell v St Pancras Borough Council* [1904]). An action for private nuisance may be brought against the occupier of the offending land, the creator of the nuisance or any person authorising the nuisance (*e.g.*, a landlord). There are *three* defences:

(1) **Consent of the claimant**—provided it is true consent (*i.e.* to both the nature and extent of the nuisance).

(2) **Prescription**—where the defendant has been committing the nuisance for more than twenty years and has done so without force, secrecy or permission, this is a defence against a claimant who has not complained during this time. However, this is of little practical application as the

time starts running from the time the particular claimant became aware of the nuisance (*Sturges v Bridgman* [1879]), and it is no defence to argue that the claimant 'came into' the nuisance.

(3) **Statutory authority**—*i.e.* where the defendant's actions are in pursuance of a statutory power or duty, though they must take all reasonable steps to minimise any nuisance.

What is "public nuisance"?

A public nuisance is an act or omission (*e.g.* obstructing the highway, keeping a brothel and polluting the public water supply) that materially affects the comfort and convenience in life of a class of Her Majesty's subjects (*Attorney General v PYA Quarries Ltd* [1957])—*i.e.* an identifiable group of the general public. Public nuisance is essentially a crime and is tried on indictment in the Crown Court. Alternatively, either the Attorney General or the relevant local council may bring a civil *relator* action on behalf of the affected public. Following a criminal or relator action, an individual who has suffered *special damage* (*i.e.* particular damage over and above that suffered by the public at large), may bring a claim for damages (*Halsey v Esso Petroleum Co Ltd* [1961]).

What is "statutory nuisance"?

Many activities have been removed from the sphere of private nuisance as a result of statutory provisions that grant wide powers to local authorities to prevent environmental damage. Many forms of pollution (notably noise and smoke pollution) are now statutory nuisances under the Public Health Act 1936, the Clean Air Act 1956 and the Control of Pollution Act 1974.

---

31. TORT: TRESPASS

What is "trespass to land"?

This is the direct and intentional interference with another's land. "Land" includes not only the land itself but also the ground beneath it, any building on it, and the airspace above to such a height as is necessary for reasonable use and enjoyment. The claimant must be in possession of the land affected. The defendant must have interfered directly with the rights of the claimant by, for example: (a) unauthorised entry; (b) remaining once asked to leave; (c) placing things on the land; (d) tunnelling under the land; (e) invading the airspace above the land. There are a number of defences that available:

(1) Statutory authority.
(2) Exercise of a public or private right.
(3) Necessity (*e.g.* where A trespasses on B's land when fleeing an assault by C).
(4) Abatement of nuisance (where A enters B's land to take reasonable steps to stop a nuisance affecting A's land).
(5) Recovery of goods (where A's goods have been wrongfully taken to B's land or are accidentally there).

What is "trespass to the person"?

There are *three* forms of trespass to the person:

(1) **Assault**—an intentional and direct act which causes the claimant to fear immediate and unlawful personal violence.
(2) **Battery**—the intentional and direct application of unlawful force on another person.
(3) **False imprisonment**—the intentional and direct restraint on another's freedom of movement. The restraint must be total—there is no imprisonment if the claimant is prevented from moving in some directions but is free to move in others (*Bird v Jones* [1845]). Similarly, there is no imprisonment where the claimant has a reasonable means of escape from the restraint. The claimant, however, need not know of the restraint at the time (*Meering v Grahame-White Aviation Co Ltd* [1920]; *Murray v Ministry of Defence* [1988])—though in such cases damages are likely to be nominal.

32. TORT: STRICT AND VICARIOUS LIABILITY

What is the rule in *Rylands v Fletcher* [1868]?

Under this rule, a person who is in occupation of land and brings onto that land something that is not naturally there, and does so for their own non-natural use, and that thing is likely to do mischief should it escape, then that person will be liable for the consequences of any such escape, even in the absence of any fault on their part. The defendant must have been using the land is some non-natural way—*i.e.* they must have been engaged in some special use bringing with it an increased danger to others, and not merely the ordinary use of land or that which is for the general benefit of the community (*Rickards v Lothian* [1913]; *Transco v Stockport MBC* [2003]). This considerably limits the scope of the rule in practice. While the thing must be likely to do mischief should it escape, this does not mean it has to be inherently dangerous, merely that it is potentially dangerous should it escape in an uncontrolled way. Also, the thing *must* escape—*i.e.* leave the confines of the defendant's land (*Read v Lyons (J) & Co Ltd* [1947]).

There are *five* main defences available:

(1) **Act of God**—where the escape is the result of natural causes without any human intervention, and such natural events were not reasonably foreseeable (*Tennent v Earl of Glasgow* [1864]).
(2) **Statutory authority.**
(3) Where the escape is due to the **unforeseeable act of a stranger** (*e.g.* a trespasser).
(4) Where the claimant had, expressly or impliedly, *consented* to the thing being brought onto the land or to its remaining there. **"Consent"** means true consent, in that the claimant was aware not only of the presence of the thing but also of its potential for mischief should it escape.
(5) Where the escape is due to the **sole fault of the claimant**. Where the escape is partly due to the fault of the claimant, *contributory negligence* will apply.

The claimant will be able to claim damages in respect of all reasonably foreseeable consequences of the escape affecting the claimant's land. This allows recovery for property damage and consequential economic loss, but *not* pure economic loss (*Cattle v Stockton Waterworks Co* [1875]) or personal injury (*Transco v Stockport MBC* [2003]). Given these various limitations and restrictions, it is best to think of the rule as a sub-species of the law of nuisance, rather than a significant form of liability in its own right (*Cambridge Water Co v Eastern Counties Leather* [1993]; *Transco v Stockport MBC* [2003]).

When does vicarious liability arise in tort?

Vicarious liability is where one person is liable for the torts of another by reason of the relationship between them. By far the most common such relationship is that of employer and employee. For such liability to arise, *two* requirements must be met:

(1) There must be a **relationship of employment**. This is for the courts, not the parties, to define, and an express contractual provision that the relationship is not one of employment will not prevail over a preponderance of other terms and factors that indicate that it is (*Mersey Docks and Harbour Board v Coggins and Griffiths (Liverpool) Ltd* [1947]). In assessing this, the courts take into account a number of factors: (a) the **issue of control** (where the *employer* controls the type and manner of performance of the work of the *employee*, the relationship is likely to be one of employment); (b) the **issue of integration** (a person whose activities are integral to the enterprise is more likely to be regarded as an employee than someone whose activities are ancillary to the enterprise or temporarily attached to it) (*Stevenson, Jordan and Harrison Ltd v Macdonald* [1952]); (c) the **method of payment**; (d) the responsibility for **providing premises, materials and equipment**; (e) any provisions for **disciplinary measures** and **dismissal** (*Mersey Docks and Harbour Board v Coggins and Griffiths (Liverpool) Ltd* [1947]).

(2) The employee's tort must be so closely connected with his employment that it would be fair and just to hold the employers vicariously liable (*Lister v Hesley Hall Ltd* [2002]), or the wrongful conduct must be so closely connected with acts the employee was authorised to do that, for the purpose of the liability of the employer to

third parties, the wrongful conduct may fairly and properly be regarded as done while acting in the ordinary course of the employee's employment (*Dubai Aluminium Co Ltd v Salaam* [2003]). That these cases have extended the scope of vicarious liability as compared to the old "course of employment" test is certain, less so is the precise scope of this new test (see *Mattis v Pollock* [2003]).

An employer will *not* normally be liable for the acts of an *independent contractor*. However, they may be liable where the contractor is in breach of a non-delegable duty binding on the employer. While the employer can delegate performance of such a duty to a contractor, they cannot delegate the duty itself and will remain personally (not vicariously) liable should the contractor breach that duty. Non-delegable duties arise in *two* main situations:

(1) Where the commissioned work involves exceptional risk to others. Here the employer will be liable for any negligence by the contractor in the performance of that work (*Holliday v National Telephone Co* [1899]) but not any collateral negligence (*Padbury v Holliday and Greenwood Ltd* [1912]).
(2) Where the employer owes the victim a duty of care for their safety and protection (*e.g.* the duty on employers to provide for the health and safety at work of their employees—*Smith v Cammell Laird & Co Ltd* [1940]; the duty on Health Authorities and hospitals for the welfare and safety of patients in their care—*Cassidy v Ministry of Health* [1951]).

33. TORT: LIABILITY FOR ANIMALS

The Animals Act 1971—Liability for dangerous animals

The keeper of a dangerous animal is strictly liable for any damage it causes (s.2). A dangerous animal is one which is not commonly domesticated in the British Islands (even though it may be domesticated overseas—*Tutin v Chipperfield Promotions Ltd* [1980]), and when fully-grown is normally likely, unless restrained, to cause severe damage or any damage it may cause is likely to be severe (s.6). The keeper is anyone who owns the animal or has it in their possession or is the head of a household of which a member under the age of 16 owns the animal or has it in their possession (s.6). If they abandon the animal, they are still regarded as the owner unless and until another person assumes ownership. Another person does not assume owner-ship merely by taking possession of an animal in order to prevent it causing damage or to return it to its owner.

The Animals Act 1971—Liability for other animals

Where damage is caused by an animal other than a dangerous animal, the keeper will be strictly liable for that damage where (s.2):

(1) The damage was of a kind that the animal, unless restrained, was likely to cause or that, if caused by the animal, was likely to be severe.
(2) The likelihood of the damage or of its being severe was due to characteristics of the animal that are not normally found in animals of the same species (*i.e.* where animals of that species are normally docile but the particular animal in question is not) or are not normally so found except at particular times or in particular circumstances (*i.e.* species of animals which are normally docile but which, in certain circumstances or at particular times, behave differently, even dangerously—see *Mirvahedy v Henley* [2003]).
(3) Those characteristics were known to the keeper.

There are *three* defences available:

(1) Contributory negligence (s.10).
(2) Sole fault of the claimant (s.5)—*e.g.* where A provokes a dog into attacking him (*Nelmes v Chief Constable for of Avon & Somerset* [1993]).
(3) Consent to the risk (s.5), although an employee (*e.g.* a zoo keeper) does *not* consent to risks incidental to their employment (s.6).

The Animals Act 1971—Liability for injury to livestock by dogs

The keeper of a dog is strictly liable where the dog causes damage by killing or injuring livestock (s.3). "Livestock" includes not only common types of farm animal but also domestic varieties of duck, geese, guinea-fowl, peacock, pigeon and quail, deer not in the wild state, and grouse, pheasants and partridges in captivity. A person may have a defence to an action for killing or injuring a dog to show that, at the material time, the dog was about to, was, or had been worrying livestock (s.9).

The Animals Act 1971—Liability for straying livestock

A person to whom livestock (excluding captive grouse, pheasants and partridges) belongs will be strictly liable where that livestock strays onto land owned or occupied by another and causes damage to the land or any property on it (s.4). The owner of the livestock will also be liable for any reasonable expenses incurred in keeping the livestock while the owner is identified or pending its return or (in certain circumstances) sale. *Three* defences are available:

(1) Sole fault of the claimant, although the fact the claimant could have prevented the damage by fencing does not, in itself, make that damage the claimant's fault (s.5).
(2) Where the straying would not have occurred but for the breach by another person of a duty to fence the land (s.5).
(3) Contributory negligence (s.10).

34. HUMAN RIGHTS

What was the "residual" approach to civil liberties?

Until recently, any discussion of the legal protection of human rights in England and Wales has taken place in a context of civil *liberties*, not civil *rights*. Freedom in English law had always been an essentially *residual* concept—one was at liberty to do everything left over once the law had said what one cannot do. This notion that one is free to do anything except that which is prohibited by law was a superficially attractive one, although its attractions are less clear when we remember that there are no legal constraints on a sovereign Parliament to enact further restrictions on even the most fundamental of freedoms. Pressure to introduce better protections and a more positive, rights-based approach led to the enactment of the Human Rights Act 1998, which incorporated the European Convention on Human Rights into English law.

What is the "European Convention on Human Rights"?

The European Convention on Human Rights was adopted by the Council of Europe in 1950. Britain was an original signatory and, since 1966, accepted the right of individual petition to the European Court of Human Rights. The rights protected by the Convention are:

➢ Article 2—the right to life
➢ Article 3—freedom from torture, inhuman or degrading treatment or punishment
➢ Article 4—freedom from slavery and forced labour
➢ Article 5—freedom of the person
➢ Article 6—the right to a fair, public and independent trial
➢ Article 7—freedom from retrospective criminal laws
➢ Article 8—the right to respect for private and family life, home and correspondence
➢ Article 9—freedom of thought, conscience and religion
➢ Article 10—freedom of expression
➢ Article 11—freedom of assembly and association
➢ Article 12—the right to marry and found a family
➢ Article 13—the right to an effective remedy before a national authority for violation of any rights or freedoms protected under the Convention
➢ Article 14—freedom from discrimination

The *First Protocol* to the Convention added:

➢ Article 1—the right to the enjoyment of private property
➢ Article 2—the right to education
➢ Article 3—the right to free elections by secret ballot

What are "absolute", "limited", and "qualified" rights?

Not all the Convention rights are absolute. The absolute rights include Articles 3, 4 and 7. Others, such as Article 5, are specifically limited by the Convention itself. Finally, others, such as Articles 8, 9, 10, and 11, may be qualified by domestic law where: (a) the qualification has its basis in law; and (b) it is necessary in a democratic society (*i.e.* it must fulfill a pressing social need in pursuit of a legitimate aim and be proportionate to that aim). Under a rights-based approach there is a presumption against restriction or qualification of Convention rights. Any qualification must be authorised by law, and in the absence of precise, specific, and detailed legal authorisation, any interference with a Convention right, however justified, will be a violation of that right.

What is the "principle of proportionality"?

Prior to the Human Rights Act 1998, government actions could only be challenged by way of judicial review if they were "irrational". However, where there has been a *prima facie* violation of a Convention right, the European Court of Human Rights adopted a more stringent standard—the principle of proportionality. This means that even if a particular policy or action which interferes with a Convention right is pursuing a legitimate aim (*e.g.* the prevention of crime), this will not be justified if the means used to achieve that aim are excessive. Since the HRA came into force in 2000, the English courts have adopted the principle of proportionality with enthusiasm.

What is the "margin of appreciation"?

In relation to some Convention rights (particularly those requiring a balance to be struck between competing considerations) the European Court of Human Rights may allow a "margin of appreciation" to the domestic authorities. This means that it may be reluctant to substitute its own views of the merits of the case for those of the national authorities in determining whether a limitation is necessary in a democratic society. Since 2000, the English courts have adopted a similar principle to that of the margin of appreciation, the "doctrine of respect", requiring courts to recognize that there are situations where the national legislature or executive are better placed to make the difficult choices between competing considerations than the national courts.

What is the position regarding the right to liberty (Article 5)?

Under current English law, state powers in this area are regulated by statute: the Police and Criminal Evidence Act 1984,

Bail Act 1976, and Criminal Justice Act 1991 (as amended). (For a more detailed examination of police powers, see Chapter 6.) The rights of people in their relations with the police are also protected by the ancient writ of *habeus corpus* (requiring detention to be justified to a court), the right to legal advice, the duty solicitor schemes, and the activities of the Independent Police Complaints Commission. Furthermore, a number of civil actions may be used to remedy any unlawful infringement of personal freedom: assault; wrongful arrest; false imprisonment; and malicious prosecution. Regarding mental health, under the Mental Health Act 1983, while a person suffering from a mental disorder can be detained against their will, specific protection is offered as the validity of any such detention (or its continuation) may be challenged before the Mental Health Review Tribunal.

What is the position regarding the right to privacy (Article 8)?

This is the one right under the Convention that was not already recognised to some degree by statute or common law. It is likely to have important consequences regarding the interception of communications, whether written, telephonic or electronic (*e.g.* emails). We should note that privacy is not limited to the home but extends, for example, to the workplace. However, the limitation of the duties under the Act to "public authorities" means that this does *not* create a general right to privacy (*e.g.* privacy from media intrusion). However, recent cases such as that involving the film stars Michael Douglas and Catherine Zeta-Jones indicate that the issue of a general right to privacy will remain a live and contentious issue for some time to come.

What is the position regarding the right to freedom of expression (Article 10)?

Freedom of expression is an essential democratic right. However, it is also one that is subject to significant restrictions under existing English law. A general level of censorship is imposed by the Obscene Publications Act 1959 and common law offences of corrupting public morals and outraging public decency. More specific powers to censor, regulate and certify exist under the Cinemas Act 1985, the Video Recordings Act 1984, and the Indecent Displays (Control) Act 1991. Television broadcasting is regulated by the Broadcasting Act 1990 and the

Broadcasting Standards Commission. Newspapers are, for the moment, subject to self-regulation by the Press Complaints Commission. This is an area that generates much controversy, and the possibility of Article 10 defences may well add to this. The Official Secrets Act 1939 protects information sensitive to national security. However, the Act has been criticised on many occasions for being too widely drawn, and a number of prosecutions (*e.g.* that of Clive Ponting in 1985) have proved controversial. There have been repeated calls for greater openness and freedom of information in government. However, the law has a difficult task here in balancing legitimate national security concerns with the equally legitimate need for a democratic government to be subject to public scrutiny. Less controversial restrictions are imposed by the law of *defamation*, designed to protect an individual's reputation from untrue and damaging allegations. The balance between the general interest in free speech and the individual's interest in protecting his good name is maintained through the availability of various defences (*e.g.* fair comment on a matter of public interest). It is likely that Article 10 will strengthen the public interest defence. Furthermore, a duty not to disclose information (personal or commercial) may exist under a contract (*e.g.* contracts of employment) or in tort—a **duty of confidentiality**.

What is the position regarding the right to freedom of assembly and association (Article 11)?

The freedom for people to associate together (*e.g.* in political parties, pressure groups or trade unions) and to assemble together (*e.g.* to hold meetings, rallies or protest marches) are essential democratic rights. However, this needs to be balanced against the need to maintain public order and to enable others to pursue their own lawful and legitimate activities. Therefore, there are restrictions on freedom of association under the Public Order Act 1936 (which outlaws quasi-military organisations and the wearing of uniforms or military insignia by political groups), and the prevention of terrorism legislation (which outlaws paramilitary groups). Regarding freedom of assembly, the Public Order Act 1986 grants the police, together with local authorities, the power to regulate protest marches, and also incorporates three specific public order offences: riot, violent disorder, and affray. Further restrictions were introduced, despite considerable public opposition, by the Criminal Justice and Public Order Act 1994 in relation to 'raves', 'travellers' and protests. It may well be the case that those facing criminal proceedings in this area will seek to raise both Article 11 and Article 10 defences. However, the increased threat of terrorism at present may well make the courts less sympathetic in this area.

What is the impact of the Human Rights Act 1998?

Convention rights are incorporated into English law by s.1. It is unlawful for a "public authority" to act in a manner incompatible with the Convention when discharging any of its functions (s.6). The term "public authority" covers *three* broad categories:

(1) Obvious public authorities such as a Minister, a Government Department or agency, local authorities, health authorities and trusts, the Armed Forces and the police.
(2) Courts and tribunals.
(3) Any person or organisation that carries out functions of a public nature. Under the Act, however, they are *only* considered a public authority in relation to their *public* functions.

Parliament is expressly excluded from the scope of the Act. This means that Parliament remains fully sovereign and free to enact incompatible legislation. The minister promoting a Bill must, before second reading, make a written statement either that, in his view, the provisions of the Bill are compatible with the Convention, or that, although not compatible, the government nevertheless wished to proceed with the Bill (s.19). However, the Act has political, as well as legal, consequences, and while it retains Parliament's legal right to enact legislation which is incompatible with the Convention, it dramatically reduces its political capacity to do so.

A person is able to rely on their Convention rights by bringing proceedings or in any proceedings brought against them (s.7). However, they may only do so if they are (or would be) a victim of the unlawful act. A "victim" is someone who is directly affected by the act in question. Victims can include companies as well as individuals and may also be relatives of the victim where a complaint is made about their death.

The courts must, so far as it is possible to do so, interpret legislation in such as way as to make it compatible with the

Convention (s.3). However, while the courts may quash decisions or actions incompatible with Convention rights, or annul delegated legislation on grounds of incompatibility, they cannot disapply an Act of Parliament (s.3), only issue a "declaration of incompatibility" (s.4). Following this, the relevant minister may amend the offending legislation by statutory instrument (Sch.2). As this involves the exceptional power to use secondary legislation to amend primary legislation, the instrument is subject to the positive affirmation procedure in Parliament (for more details on this procedure, see Chapter 2). A court may, following a violation of the Convention by a public authority, grant such relief or remedy, or make such order as it considers just and appropriate (s.8). However, the court may only award damages where, taking into account all the circumstances of the case (including any other relief or remedy granted or order made), it is satisfied that damages are necessary to ensure just satisfaction for the victim.

35. THE IDEA OF LAW: LAW AND MORALITY

What are legal and moral codes?

While legal and moral codes are both concerned with establishing rules or norms of behaviour, and therefore have many similar features, there are also important differences:

Moral Codes	Legal Codes
• General statements of principle	• Precise rules of conduct
• Voluntary subscription	• Compulsory subscription
• Informal enforcement	• Formal enforcement
• Concerned with how people *ought* to behave	• Concerned with how people *shall* behave

The relationship between law and morality exists for both *historical* and *functional* reasons. Historically, legal codes tend to emerge from moral codes. In primitive societies, there is often little or no difference between the two. However, as the society becomes more diverse (socially, culturally, economically and morally) the need for a distinct and universally applicable set of rules (a legal system) emerges. Functionally, both law and morality are used to perform similar social tasks—to preserve order and maintain acceptable standards of behaviour through the promotion and enforcement of rules and principles. Thus, it is not surprising that the relationship between law and morality is a complex one, and that moral influences pervade much of the law.

However, this is not to suggest all that may be regarded as immoral is necessarily illegal (*e.g.* adultery) or vice versa (*e.g.* parking offences).

How has morality influenced in English law?

Moral notions form the background or context of many aspects of English law, with its concerns for the protection of the person, property, the family, etc. However, as noted above, the legal rules will tend to be more specific and precise than their moral counterparts. In the vast majority of instances, this moral context to the law is uncontroversial. Indeed, it is positively beneficial, as enhances the legitimacy of the law and encourages the observance of legal rules. However, problems may arise where moral issues become foregrounded, rather than merely providing a background context—*i.e.* where the law is used specifically to enforce particular moral positions. In the legislative sphere, examples include the Abortion Act 1967 and the Obscene Publications Act 1956. In the judicial sphere, examples include the common law offences of conspiracy to corrupt public morals (*Shaw v DPP* [1962]; *Knuller (Publishing, Printing and Promotions) Ltd v DPP* [1973]) and conspiracy to outrage public decency (*R v Gibson* [1991]). This foregrounding of particular moral positions becomes problematic where the social consensus on that issue has broken down or fragmented, and the more diverse a society becomes, the greater the potential for fragmentation.

How should the law approach moral issues?

There are *three* main approaches to issues of moral controversy:

(1) **The libertarian approach**—the law should not interfere in private behaviour except in order to prevent harm to others. However, it is sometimes difficult to identify the

boundaries between private and public conduct and the limits of harm (*e.g.* drug use may be a 'private' activity but can have 'public' and 'harmful' consequences, such as additional burdens on the public health system and criminal activity to feed the habit).

(2) **The liberal approach**—this is typified by the Wolfenden Committee on Homosexual Offences and Prostitution, which reported in 1957. The Committee's view was that the law should not interfere in private behaviour except where necessary to preserve public order and decency, to protect against the offensive and injurious, and to safe-guard individuals (particularly the most vulnerable) against corruption and exploitation. However, difficulties arise with this approach due to the subjective nature of the criteria advanced—by whose standards is something to be judged "offensive" or "injurious"?

(3) **The duty/aspiration approach**—this more satisfactory approach distinguishes between the morality of duty and the morality of aspiration. The morality of duty indicates the standard of behaviour that most people would be prepared to tolerate (*i.e.* the bare minimum level of acceptable conduct). By contrast, the morality of aspira-tion indicates the standard of behaviour to which most people should aspire. While the law may be employed to enforce the morality of duty, it cannot and should not be used to enforce the morality of aspiration (*i.e.* it is legitimate to use the law to prevent people behaving badly, but not to use it in an attempt to force people to behave virtuously). This approach can be seen it in the famous "neighbour principle" advanced by Lord Atkin in *Donoghue v Stevenson* [1932].

---

36. THE IDEA OF LAW: LAW AND JUSTICE

What is 'justice'?

"Justice" is extremely difficult to define. Not only are there different definitions of justice, but the question "what is justice?'' means different things in different contexts—Is a particular law just? Is the legal system just? Does the combination of law and system produce a just result? Some of the major theories of justice are:

(1) **Aristotlean justice**—this was one of the earliest attempts to formulate a theory of justice. Aristotle argued that the basis of justice is fairness, and that this takes two forms: (a) **distributive justice**, whereby the law is used to ensure social benefits and burdens are fairly distributed throughout society; and (b) **corrective justice**, whereby the legal system acts to correct attempts by individuals to disturb this fair distribution.

(2) **Utilitarian theory**— the central principle of utilitarianism is that society should be organised to achieve the greatest happiness for the greatest number. Thus, according to a utilitarian approach, a law is just where it brings about a net gain in happiness for the majority, even if this is at the cost of increased distress or unhappiness to a minority. However, it is this willingness to trade the unhappiness of the minority against the happiness of the majority that liberal theory finds most objectionable in this approach.

(3) **Liberal (or natural rights) theory**—liberal theory judges the justice of any form of social organisation by the extent it protects its minorities and most vulnerable groups. Therefore, they tend to incorporate notions of natural rights to which all people are entitled. However, this approach has its own problems, not least in establishing agreement over the content and extent of any list of ''natural'' rights. For example, the right to vote is now regarded as an essential and universal right. However, for many years this was subject to a property qualification, and was not one to which women were entitled until this century.

(4) **Libertarian (or market-based) theory**—libertarian theory argues that intervention in the natural (or market) distribution of advantages (as required by the other theories) is an unjust interference with individual rights. Libertarian analysis only permits very limited intervention to prevent unjust distribution (*e.g.* through theft and fraud). However, such a narrow approach is open to many of the same objections as the utilitarian approach.

Therefore, it may be argued that the question of abstract justice seems to be as much a political as philosophical one.

How does the English Legal System achieve justice?

While whether a particular law is just is essentially a political question, consideration must also be given to whether the system is just, and whether it produces a just outcome. This involves both *formal justice* (regarding the system) and *substantive justice* (regarding outcomes):

(1) **Formal justice** requires a system of independent tribunals for the administration of law and the resolution of disputes, as is recognised by Article 6 of the European Convention on Human Rights, now incorporated into English law by the Human Rights Act 1998. The formal trial and appellate courts, together with the various forms of alternative dispute resolution, ensure the English legal system largely meets this requirement. Formal justice also requires these institutions follow known and fair rules and procedures. Again, this is met through the rules of due process and fair procedure, rules regarding the admissibility of evidence, limitation periods etc, that apply in the English courts. Finally, it is important that any citizen with a grievance has access to these institutions. Here more needs to be done to ensure this, particularly for the poorest and least-advantaged sections of our society (see Chapter 14).

(2) **Substantive justice**—the English legal system has a variety of mechanisms to ensure just outcomes. Regarding common law, the principle of stare decisis, together with devices such as overruling and distinguishing, enable the courts to work towards both the just development of the common law itself and a just outcome in any given case. The courts may also turn to the principles of Equity where the strict application of common law rules would lead to injustice. Furthermore, where the courts are unable to resolve such issues, because they are dealing with statute or they have reached the limits of proper common law development, Parliament may act to remedy matters through legislation. It is this capacity to be self-correcting that is one of the most important aspects of the English legal system's ability to ensure just outcomes.

Given the variety of subjective, vague, and sometimes contradictory notions of abstract justice, the best that any *system* of justice can hope to achieve is *justice according to law*. This is a task the English legal system is well-equipped to perform, not least in its capacity for development and self-correction.

37. THE IDEA OF LAW: THE JUDGE AS LAW-MAKER

How are judges involved in law-making?

Judges are involved in the law-making process in a number of ways: (a) participation in various advisory committees, commissions and inquiries; (b) participation of the Law Lords in the legislative business of the House of Lords, though limited by convention to law reform measures and issues of legal technicality; (c) their role as the definitive interpreters of legislation; and (d) their responsibility for the development and evolution of the common law.

What approaches can judges take to law-making?

For many years the judiciary denied any law-making role, arguing they merely declared the law as laid down by statute or fundamental principles of common law. However, the modern judiciary has increasingly abandoned the fiction of this declaratory approach and acknowledged they do indeed exercise a law-making role. Lee argues there are *three* main factors that influence judicial law-making:

(1) The previous history of legislative development.
(2) The consequences of the present law and the likely consequences of any given change.
(3) The judiciary's own perception of the proper limits of its law-making role.

In relation to (3), Harris contrasts *two* judicial "styles":

(1) **Formal Style**, characterised by caution and a tendency to rely on formal devices such as distinguishing.
(2) **Grand Style**, characterised by boldness and a willingness to recognise issues of policy as well as principle.

Paterson observed similar variations in judicial approaches to "hard" cases:

(1) **The positive response** (similar to the Grand Style).
(2) **The adaptive response** (similar to the Formal Style).
(3) **To withdraw** on the basis that the proposed change is properly one for Parliament rather than the judges to make.

The majority of judges adopt the Formal or adaptive position. However, a minority, particularly in the higher courts, have always followed a more adventurous path. These different styles or responses highlight the distinction between law-making according to established principles and law-making according to policy. It is generally felt judges should confine their attention to issues of principle, as these are seen as politically neutral. It is for Parliament to determine the political acceptability of any development according to principle. However, this is something of a false distinction as the boundary between principle and policy is easily blurred. Furthermore, Parliament cannot be expected to legislate for everything. In a common law system, judges not only have scope for law-making but, as Lord Lane pointed out in *R v R (rape: marital exemption)* [1991], are under a duty to do so, provided this is done in the context of a proper regard for the superior role of Parliament. In this respect, Lord Devlin drew a distinction between:

(1) **Activist** law-making—changing the law *in response to* changes in the social consensus.
(2) **Dynamic** law-making—changing the law *in order to promote* change in the social consensus.

He argued that while it was proper for judges to engage in activist law-making, dynamic law-making should be left to Parliament. He also pointed out judges had far less scope and authority for law-making when dealing with statute than with the common law. Therefore, there are three main constraints on judicial law-making:

(1) Judges are bound by the rules of precedent when dealing with the common law.
(2) Judges are bound by the rules of statutory interpretation when dealing with statutes.

(3) Judges are bound by their own perception of the proper limits of the judiciary's law-making role and of the superior role of Parliament in the law-making partnership with the courts.

How could judges discharge this role more effectively?

A number of reforms could enhance the effectiveness of this role:

(1) **A formal procedure** by which the courts could refer issues to Parliament when it is felt that further development is beyond the scope of legitimate judicial law-making.
(2) The introduction of an **independent advisor** in the appellate courts to perform a similar role to the Advocate General in the Court of Justice of the European Union.
(3) The provision of **research attorneys** to the judiciary in the appellate courts. Following a pilot scheme in 1997, judges in the Court of Appeal are now provided with *Judicial Assistants* (appointed on a full or part-time basis for up to one year). In 2000, this was extended to the House of Lords with the appointment of *Legal Assistants* on one-year contracts to assist the Law Lords.

---

38. THE IDEA OF LAW: FAULT AND LIABILITY

What is the relationship between fault and criminal liability?

The criminal law is the most obvious candidate for fault-based liability. A person should not be found guilty of a crime and deprived of their liberty without proof of individual fault. This insistence upon fault can be seen in the general requirements of liability—the *actus reus* and *mens rea*. We can also argue the absence of fault is the underlying rationale for the various general defences. Finally, the degree of fault shown is a major determining factor in sentencing.

Regarding the *actus reus*, the general requirement of a positive, voluntary act and the limited liability for omissions are evidence of the need for fault, as is the requirement of causation in relation to result crimes (if the defendant did not cause the unlawful consequence, it is not his fault and hence he is not liable).

The different states of mind employed to construct the *mens rea* of different offences demonstrate the relationship between degree of fault and liability. Generally, a person can only be convicted of the most serious offences on proof of intention to commit that offence. Less serious offences may be committed recklessly, and minor offences, frequently of a regulatory nature, can be committed negligently.

Some defences, such as automatism, operate by showing lack of fault through the involuntary nature of the defendant's conduct. Others, such as insanity and intoxication, operate by establishing a lack of mental control or awareness on the part of the defendant. Others, such as duress and self-defence, operate by establishing that the defendant's conduct was justified or should be excused.

Finally, the partial defences to murder, such as provocation and diminished responsibility, demonstrate a lesser degree of fault resulting in conviction for the lesser offence of manslaughter. The degree of fault on the part of the defendant also plays a very significant role in sentencing. Both the type of sentence imposed (custodial, community or fine) and its severity is in large part determined by the degree of fault shown by the defendant. This can also be seen in the impact of both aggravating and mitigating factors. This is why some are opposed to the use of minimum and mandatory sentences, as they break the relationship between the degree of fault present in the offence committed and the sentence imposed. However, there is a limited role for strict liability in the criminal law. In relation to both regulatory offences and offences of social danger, the interests of society as a whole, determined by Parliament (the courts are extremely reluctant to create strict liability offences at common law, or even to recognise them in statute) can sometimes justify the imposition of liability without fault. Nevertheless, the degree of fault still plays an important role in determining the sentence following conviction.

What is the relationship between fault and tortious liability?

The aim of tort is to provide a remedy (usually in the form of financial compensation) for the victims of wrongs, and fault on the part of the defendant is the device most generally used to attach liability for this. Negligence liability is clearly dependent upon proof of fault (a failure to take reasonable care) on the part of the defendant. While nuisance liability may sometimes take on the appearance of strict liability, it remains essentially fault-based—the defendant is liable for failing to meet the reasonable expectations of his neighbours.

Furthermore, the general defences in tort have their basis in the absence or lesser degree of fault in the same way as those in criminal law. However, it is true to say that strict liability plays a larger role in tort than criminal law. This is generally in areas where there are overriding social concerns in encouraging the greatest possible (rather than merely reasonable) care (*e.g.* in ensuring products are safe). Hence, strict liability in tort is to some extent deployed regarding defective products, the keeping of animals, and certain forms of industrial and environmental activity. Those engaged in such activities will frequently choose, and are sometimes obliged, to insure against liability.

Furthermore, while there are clear arguments in favour of a fault-based system of liability regarding torts such as negligence, the present insistence of fault in these areas can place significant obstacles in the path of the very people the system is intended to benefit. This has given rise to increasing concerns, particularly regarding personal injury cases.

What are the arguments in favour of fault-based liability in Tort?

- ☑ It is a just approach to the apportioning of liability. Where fault indicates the person responsible for the damage, justice requires that person compensate the victim. However, it is at least questionable whether justice requires that in the absence of fault, the loss should be borne by the blameless victim.
- ☑ The requirement of fault acts as an incentive to take care, as if liability were to be imposed regardless of fault, people would take less care as no advantage would accrue to the careful. However, this rests on the dubious assumption that people take care to avoid injuring others solely or largely in order to avoid legal liability.

☑ The requirement of fault deters deliberate self-maiming. It is true that in jurisdictions with no-fault systems there have been instances of people injuring themselves in order to obtain compensation. However, the numbers currently denied access to compensation by the requirement of fault far exceed any likely number of self-maiming claims.

☑ To move to a no-fault system would involve a massive extension of liability and place an excessive burden on defendants. Whether this would in fact result depends upon how the system is funded, but even under the present arrangements the bulk of any additional costs would be spread throughout society at large, through a rise in insurance costs, rather than falling directly upon individuals.

What are the arguments against fault-based liability in Tort?

☒ The practical consequences of a fault-based system are unacceptable. The difficulties in establishing both fault and causation make the system a "forensic lottery". Furthermore, it is an extremely inefficient mechanism. The Pearson Commission (1978) found the administrative costs of the tort system were equivalent to 85 per cent of sums paid in compensation, amounting to 45 per cent of the total compensation and administration costs. By contrast, compensation via the social security system would involve administration costs amounting to only 11 per cent of the total, providing a substantially cheaper and quicker compensation mechanism.

☒ A fault-based system is wrong in principle as well as practice. While fault may provide a good reason for taking money from defendants, it is an inappropriate basis to decide which victims will receive compensation. Furthermore, except where there is joint liability or contributory negligence, the present system takes no account of the degree of fault. Also, because the aim is to compensate the victim, the assessment of damages takes no account of the defendant's ability to pay (unlike the criminal law when assessing the level of fines). Finally, the present system has itself recognised these failings by allowing (and even in some cases making compulsory) the use of loss-distribution devices such as insurance and developing notions such as vicarious liability.

What is the alternative?

The main alternative is a no-fault compensation system, financed either through compulsory private insurance or public revenues. Critics of such schemes often point to the fact that levels of compensation are lower than those provided by damages at common law. However, a system that ensures adequate compensation for all would seem preferable to a system that provides full compensation for only a few.

What is the relationship between fault and contractual liability?

Contractual liability is essentially strict. The reasons for this are pragmatic rather than based on any clear difference of principle—it would be absurd that every time someone was supplied with a defective product, they had to discover whose fault it was. Having said this, there are circumstances where the fault does play a part in contract law—*e.g.*:

(1) The remedies available to a misrepresentee are, in part, determined by the degree of fault on the part of the misrepresentor.
(2) Where a contract is void for illegality, the normal principles of restitution will not apply.
(3) Where a contract is discharged by frustration, the law seeks to achieve a fair apportioning of loss between two innocent parties.

---

39. SUCCESS IN THE EXAMINATION

Whether you are writing an essay, answering questions based on source material provided by the examining board, or answering a 'case study' or 'problem' style question, it is essential to bear in mind the assessment objectives of the course, as the marks available are awarded according to how well you meet these objectives:

Assessment Objective	What you are expected to do
AO1	Recall, select, deploy and develop knowledge and understanding of legal principles accurately and by means of example and citation
AO2	Analyse legal material, issues and situations, and evaluate and apply the appropriate legal rules and principles
AO3	Present a logical and coherent argument and communicate relevant material in a clear and effective manner using appropriate legal terminology

The most important thing to remember when answering an essay question is to ensure you answer the *specific* question set, and *not* merely recite a stock answer or write all you can remember about the particular topic concerned. It is also essential to **plan** your answer carefully before you begin. A clear plan is vital to ensure relevance, accuracy, clarity and logical argument (AO3). A2 questions generally require both description (AO1) and evaluation (AO2). AS level questions will tend to be more descriptive (AO1), but will still require simple evaluation (AO2).

In answering 'case study' or 'problem' style questions, you should consider using the following approach:

(1) Read the facts and all the questions carefully—use the questions to help you identify the relevant issues and facts.

(2) List the important and relevant facts, in the order in which they happen, together with the issue(s) each raises in a facts and issues table.

(3) Answer each question in full, referring to the facts and issues table, using the three-stage approach: (a) **identify** and **define** the issues raised; (b) **state** and **explain** the relevant rules of law (with authorities); **apply** the rules to the facts and **suggest** the likely outcome.

Whatever the type of question you are answering, there are *four key watchwords (P.A.C.E.)* to bear in mind:

- **Precision** (ensure you state the law accurately and precisely).

- **Authorities** (ensure you support your points by reference to relevant cases and statutes).
- **Clarity** (of both expression and structure).
- **Examples** (illustrate your points wherever possible with examples, either drawn from real cases or hypothetical).

To prepare for your examinations, it is important to find out as much as possible about what to expect. You should obtain copies of the specification for the Board you are studying. These can be found on the boards' websites (*www.aqa.org.uk*, *www.ocr.org.uk*). You should also obtain copies of past papers, mark schemes, and Chief Examiner's reports, as these can help you understand the examiner's expectations, how best you can meet them, and the sorts of common mistakes to avoid.

As for the exam itself, make sure you know when it is, where it is, what time it starts and what time you have to be there. You should also know how long the exam lasts and how many questions you have to answer. This will enable you to have a time plan for the exam. It's essential that you stay in control of the exam—do not let it take control of you! You should also make a list of all the things you have to take with you—identification, statement of entry, pen, spare pen, etc. Make sure you follow the instructions on the exam paper, answering the correct number of questions for each section of the paper.

Once the exam is over, turn your attention to your next one—do not dwell on lengthy *post mortems* of the one you have just done. Once all your exams are over, relax—if you have been studying properly you will have earned a rest. Then try and forget about it all until the results are published. If you have been working hard and done your best, no-one can criticise you. Hopefully, you will have enjoyed your course and achieved the result you deserve. Good luck!

INDEX